Introduction to the iPad and iPhone

I0004855

The Mail App

© 2018 iTandCoffee

iOS 11 Edition

Special Sales and Supply Queries

For any information about buying this title in bulk quantities, or for supply of this title for educational or fund-raising purposes, contact iTandCoffee on **1300 885 420** or email **enquiry@itandcoffee.com.au**.

iTandCoffee classes and private appointments

For queries about classes and private appointments with iTandCoffee, call **1300 885 420** or email **enquiry@itandcoffee.com.au.**

iTandCoffee operates in and around Glen Iris, Victoria in Australia.

Introducing iTandCoffee ...

iTandCoffee is a Melbourne-based business that was founded in 2012, by IT professional Lynette Coulston.

Lynette and the staff at iTandCoffee have a passion for helping others - especially women of all ages - to enter and navigate the new, and often daunting, world of technology.

At iTandCoffee, **patience is our virtue.**

You'll find a welcoming smile, a relaxed cup of tea or coffee, and a genuine enthusiasm for helping you to gain the confidence to use and enjoy your technology.

With personalised appointments and small, friendly classes – either at our bright, comfortable, cafe-style shop in Glen Iris or at your place - we offer a brand of technology support and education that is so hard to find.

At iTandCoffee, you won't find young 'techies' who speak in a foreign language and move at a pace that leaves you floundering and 'bamboozled'!

Our focus is on helping you to use your technology in a way that enhances your personal and/or professional life – to feel more informed, organised, connected and entertained!

Call on iTandCoffee for help with all sorts of technology – Apple, Windows, iCloud, Evernote, Dropbox, all sorts of other Apps (including Microsoft Office products), getting you set up on the internet, setting up a printer, and so much more.

iTandCoffee
Relax, we'll help you get iT

Here are just some of the topics covered in our regular classes at iTandCoffee:

- Introduction to the iPad and iPhone
- The next step on your iPad and iPhone
- Bring your Busy Life under Control using the iPad and iPhone
- Getting to know your Mac
- Understanding and using iCloud
- An Organised Life with Evernote
- Taking and Managing photos on the iPhone and iPad
- Travel with your iPad, iPhone and other technology.
- Keeping kids safe on the iPad, iPhone and iPod Touch.
- Staying Safe Online

The iTandCoffee website (itandcoffee.com.au) offers a wide variety of resources for those brave enough to venture online to learn more: handy hints for iPad, iPhone and Mac; videos and slideshows of iTandCoffee classes; guides on a range of topics; a blog covering all sorts of topical events.

We also produce a regular Handy Hint newsletter full of information that is of interest to our clients and subscribers.

Hopefully, that gives you a bit of a picture of iTandCoffee and what we are about. Please don't hesitate to iTandCoffee on 1300 885 420 to discuss our services or to make a booking.

We hope you enjoy this guide and find its contents informative and useful. Please feel free to offer feedback at feedback@itandcoffee.com.au.

Regards,

Lynette Coulston (iTandCoffee Owner)

Introduction to the iPad and iPhone
The Mail App

Table of Contents

Introduction to the iPad and iPhone

The Mail App

Table of Contents

Introduction to the iPad and iPhone
The Mail App

Table of Contents

Introduction to the iPad and iPhone
The Mail App

Table of Contents

Introduction

Sending, receiving and managing emails on your iPad and iPhone is achieved using the **Mail app** – one of the standard set of apps provided by Apple.

Just tap on the envelope icon on your Home screen to open the Mail app.

But before you do ...

For the Mail app to be able to access your email account, you must first tell your device about your email account by 'adding' it to your iPad or iPhone.

I often get asked why this doesn't just happen when you tell your iPad or iPhone about your Apple ID, which is often the same email address as used by your email account.

This is because your email account is quite a separate thing to your Apple account, iTunes account and iCloud account (unless you use an '@icloud.com' or '@me.com' for your iCloud email address – in which case your email setup WILL be done when you sign in to your iCloud).

Even though you may have used your email address as your Apple ID, this is just so that you could give a unique name for your Apple account and provide a way for Apple to contact you via email.

It does not 'install' that email account on your iPad/iPhone. You must do this separately by telling your device about your email provider, then providing your email address and password.

Let's start by looking briefly at how to do this, so that you can start sending and receiving your emails on your device.

Setting up your email account

If you already have your email account installed on your iPad or iPhone, you may wish to skip this section. Just remember that you are not limited to a single email account on your device and can always add another one at any time.

Once it is set up, most of the settings for your Mail account are located in the **Mail** option within the **Settings** application. We'll explore these later.

However, the option to set up an email account on your device is not located within the **Mail** option (as it was in iOS 10).

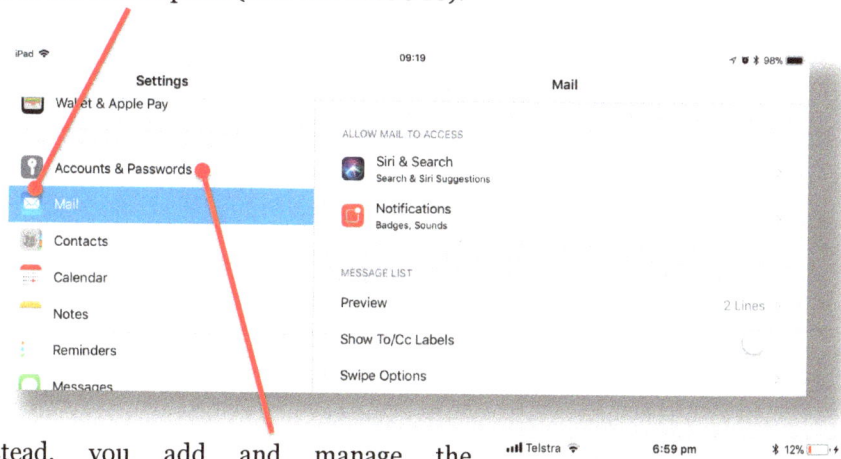

Instead, you add and manage the configuration details of all your Mail accounts in the **Accounts & Passwords** option.

To add an email account to your iPad or iPhone, select the '**Add Account**' option in the **Accounts & Passwords** setting.

There are differences in the setup process, depending on the provider of your email account – whether your provider is one of the standard set provided, or requires more customised setup.

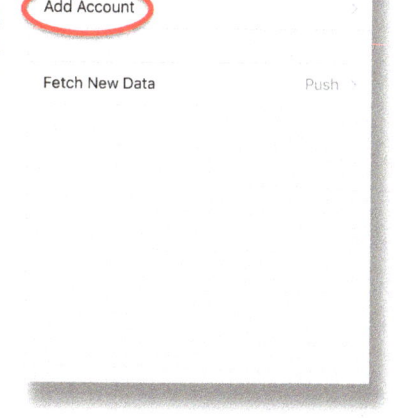

Setting up your email account

If your email provider is shown in list of options

You will be offered a selection of common email account types from which to choose.

If you see your email provider in the list, touch on it.

If you have a Gmail account, tap Google.

If you have a Hotmail or Live account, choose the Outlook.com account option. (This is because Hotmail is now part of Microsoft, and their mail accounts are known as 'Outlook' accounts).

Tapping on the **'Google'**, **'YAHOO!'** or **'Outlook.com'** options will redirect you to that email service's website where you can input your information in the fields provided and very easily set up the connection to your email account.

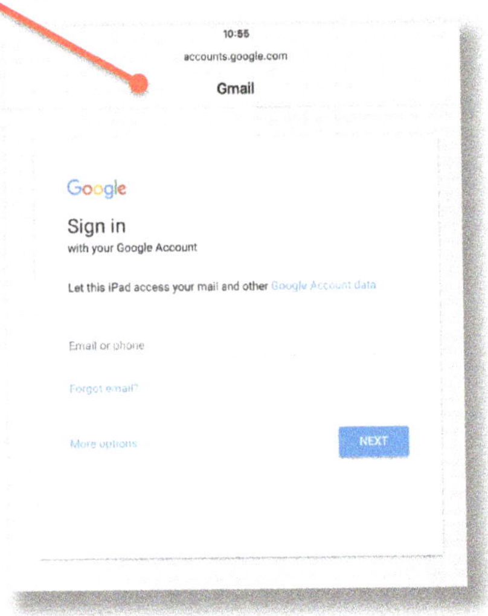

Touching **'iCloud'**, **'Exchange'** or **'AOL'** will give you a screen that requires entry of your Name (i.e. first name and surname), your email address and your password. A Description field will be automatically filled in but can be changed to a name that better identifies your account. This is the account name that will appear in your Mail app.

Once the account information has been correctly entered, a confirmation screen will appear.

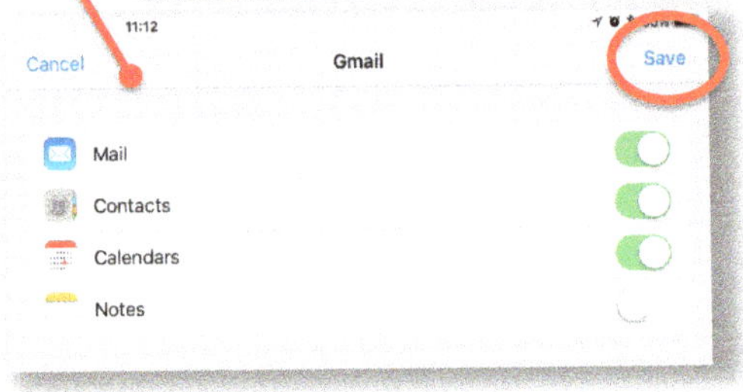

On this screen, you can select what aspects of the account are active by tapping on the sliders next to each option. This determines whether information contained within the account is transferred to your device and sync'd with that mail account.

Press Save to finishing setting up the email account on your device.

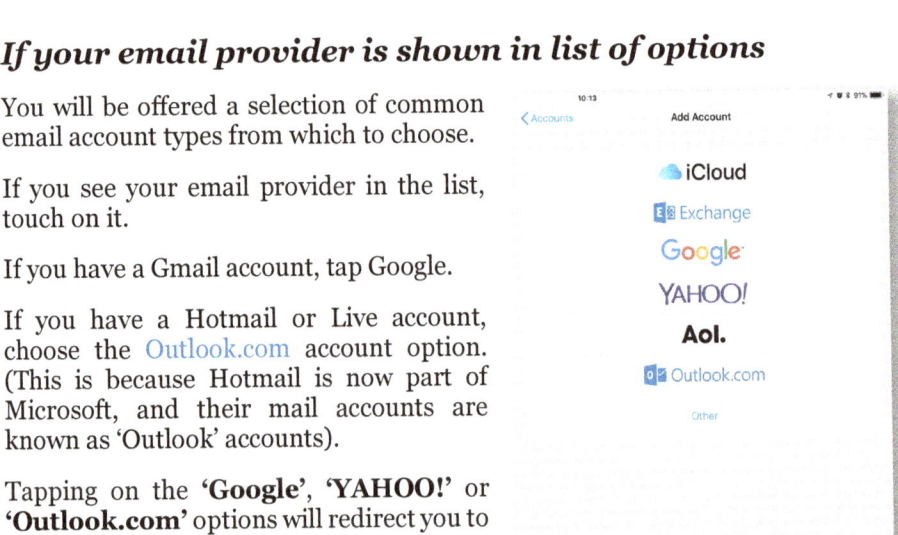

12

Setting up your email account

If you don't see your email provider in the list

If, for example, you are with Bigpond, Optusnet, TPG or some other provider – or if you have your own hosted email account - choose the Other option at the end of the list, then touch on **Add Mail Account** at the top.

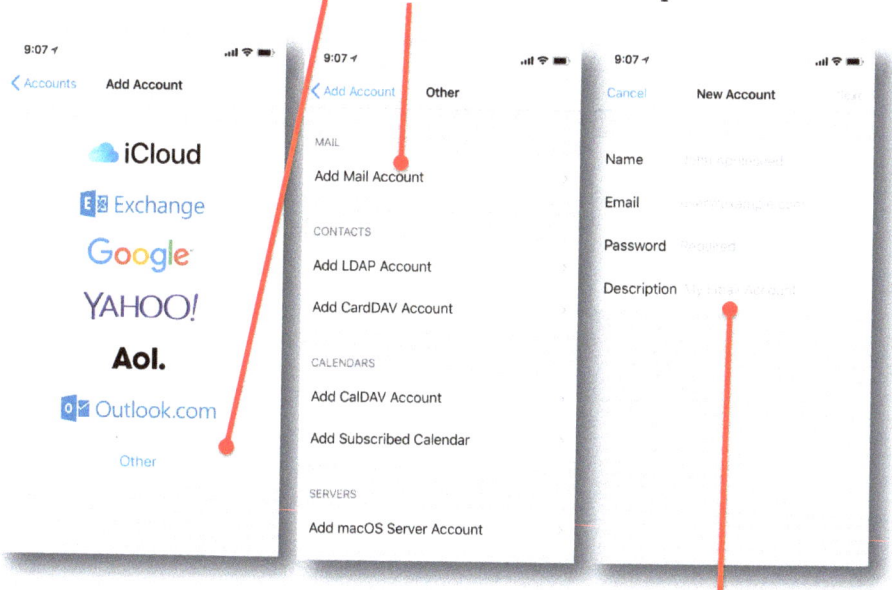

As for the other types of email address, you will have to provide your name, email address, the account's password and a description for the account (which will be given a default valued that you can change if you like).

Once you have done that and selected Next at top right, and the account setup will hopefully complete automatically without a glitch!

Unfortunately, this is not always the case, and some 'tweaking' of the settings is sometimes required to get your mail up and running.

There are so many different types of email account – Bigpond, Optusnet, TPG, private and business email addresses – and setup of these may differ and require

Setting up your email account

some more expert assistance. There may be some customisation of settings like 'incoming mail server', 'outgoing mail server', 'ports' and/or 'Use SSL'. We'll cover where to adjust these more advanced settings towards the end of this guide.

Googling words like "iOS mail settings for Bigpond" can help you determine what the setup should look like. Your internet provider may be able to guide you through the required setup over the phone or at their store (if they have one).

Feel free to contact iTandCoffee to make an appointment - we can help if you have any issues with installing your mail account.

You are not limited to one email account

If you have more than one email address, you can add one or more other email accounts to your iPad or iPhone by following the above steps again.

Once your mail account is successfully installed on your iPad or iPhone, your emails will start downloading to your device's Mail app.

We look next at how your emails are organized in Mail – into **Mailboxes**.

Exploring Mailboxes

When you touch on your **Mail** app on the Home Screen to access your emails, the screen that you see will depend on whether you have previously used the Mail app, the Mailbox that you were previously looking at, the device that you are using (i.e. iPhone vs iPad) and whether your iPad is in 'portrait' or 'landscape' mode.

First let's make sure we are looking at the same thing!

If your **Mail** app has opened into your **Inbox** (or any other 'Mailbox'), simply tap the < option in the top left corner to be taken to your **Mailboxes** view.

(The word that appears on the right of this < symbol will change, depending on which Mailbox you are currently viewing.)

The standard mailboxes

Let's first understand the main set of 'mailboxes' that hold all your email – each of which will only appear if you have any emails that fit that category

Inbox
Emails that have been sent to you.

Sent
Email that you have sent to others

Drafts
Emails that you have started drafting, then cancelled before sending and chosen to 'Save Draft'.

Bin
Emails that you have deleted.

Junk
Emails that have been automatically categorised as 'SPAM'/'JUNK' by your email provider, or that you have chosen to 'mark as Junk'.

Outbox
Emails that you have Sent, but that have not yet been sent from your device – perhaps due to a lack of internet connection, or a problem with the 'outgoing mail server' for your mail account.

Exploring Mailboxes

Some special mailboxes

Updates to iOS versions have delivered some flexibility around what mailboxes you see in your **Mailboxes** list.

You have the ability to 'turn on and off' certain mailboxes. Additionally, some special (and very useful) mailboxes called - 'smart mailboxes' - have been added. **Smart Mailboxes** are mailboxes whose contents are automatically determined.

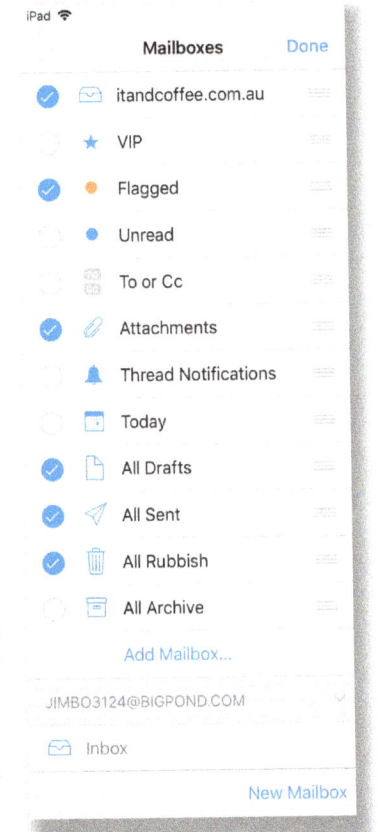

Let's look at the list of these 'smart mailboxes' that are available:

VIP
Emails from people that you have nominated to be VIP - we'll cover how to nominate your VIPs later in the guide.

Flagged
Emails that you have 'flagged' to remind you they they are important or perhaps need following- up – we'll cover how to do this shortly.

Unread
Emails that you have not yet touched on to read – they will be the ones with a 'blue dot' next to them.

Today
Emails in your Inbox that have been received today only.

To or CC
List of emails that you have received but includes a 'To' and 'Cc' label to show whether the message was sent to you, or you were Cc'd.

Attachments
Lists all emails that have attachments, such as a document, PDF or photo.

Thread Notifications
Shows all emails relating to a 'thread' that you have asked to be notified about (we'll cover this later)

Exploring Mailboxes

If you have more than one email account, you may also have the following 'smart mailboxes' available:

All Inboxes, All Sent, All Drafts, All Rubbish, All Archive

These mailboxes combine the equivalent mailboxes of your separate mail accounts into a single mailbox – so that you don't have to look at each account's mailbox separately. You may also see All Archive if you have certain types of email account.

But I am missing some 'Mailboxes'

The list of Mailboxes that you see can be customised to include or exclude <u>any</u> of the above-mentioned mailboxes.

In fact, you can sometimes find that you accidentally 'turn off' one of your essential mailboxes – for example, your Inbox - and are left wondering where it has gone!

To adjust the list of mailboxes that you see, just touch on the word Edit at top right of the Mailboxes list.

After selecting Edit, you will see your screen mailbox list change to include some extra items, and each item will have a circle on the left.

Just tap in the circle next to a mailbox to tick or untick it – only those that are ticked will appear in your Mailboxes list when you choose Done.

You can change the order of your mailboxes in this top section by touching and holding on the 'three lines' symbol ═ on the right of the mailbox name, then dragging it upwards or downwards into the required position.

Choose Done when you have finished selecting, unselecting and re-arranging your Mailboxes.

If desired, you can add further 'favourite' mailboxes to this first section – for example if you have created your own personal mailboxes in your Gmail account for 'filing away' correspondence.

The Add Mailbox option at the bottom allows for the selection of which other Mailbox/es you would like to see in this 'favourites' list.

Exploring Mailboxes

The sections shown in Mailboxes

If you only have one email account, your Mailboxes list will have two 'sections'.

The top section will contain your Inbox and any of the 'Smart Mailboxes' that you have 'ticked' in Edit mode.

The second section will show all the other Mailboxes in your email account – your Drafts, Sent, Junk, Bin, Archive, and any personal Mailboxes that you have created. As mentioned earlier, you'll only see Drafts, Send, Junk, Bin and Archive if you have any emails of that type of on your device.

(We'll cover how to create personal Mailboxes later.)

If you have added more than one email account on your device, you will see more than two 'sections' in your Mailboxes list.

The top section will include your special '**All Inboxes**' smart Mailbox, which will combine all mail from all your different accounts Inbox, listed by 'date received.

Included also in the first section will be each of your email accounts' inboxes – so that you can just view the incoming mail for a specific email account.

Also included also in that section will be the **Smart Mailboxes** that you have 'ticked' in Edit mode.

The subsequent sections will then show the set of Mailboxes associated with each individual email account.

In the example shown here, there will be sections for my Gmail (circled on right), iCloud, Bigpond, and iTandCoffee accounts, showing Drafts, Sent, Junk, Bin, Archive, and any personal Mailboxes that I have created for each of these accounts.

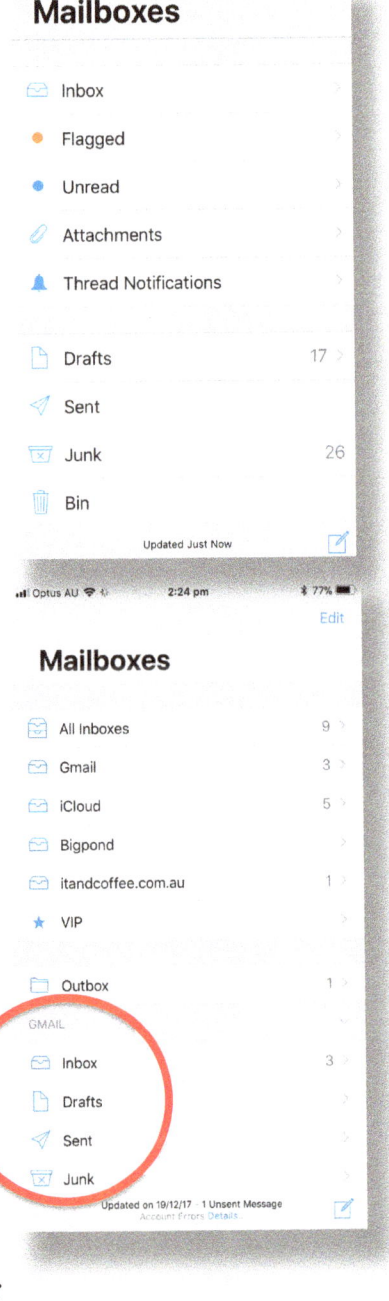

Your Email Toolbar

When you have a selected email in view, you will see a 'toolbar' at the top of the screen on an iPad, and the top and bottom of the screen on an iPhone.

If this toolbar is greyed or not visible, just touch on a message to read it, and the options will become visible and available.

Here is a guide to the options and their functions. We will refer to the symbols throughout this guide.

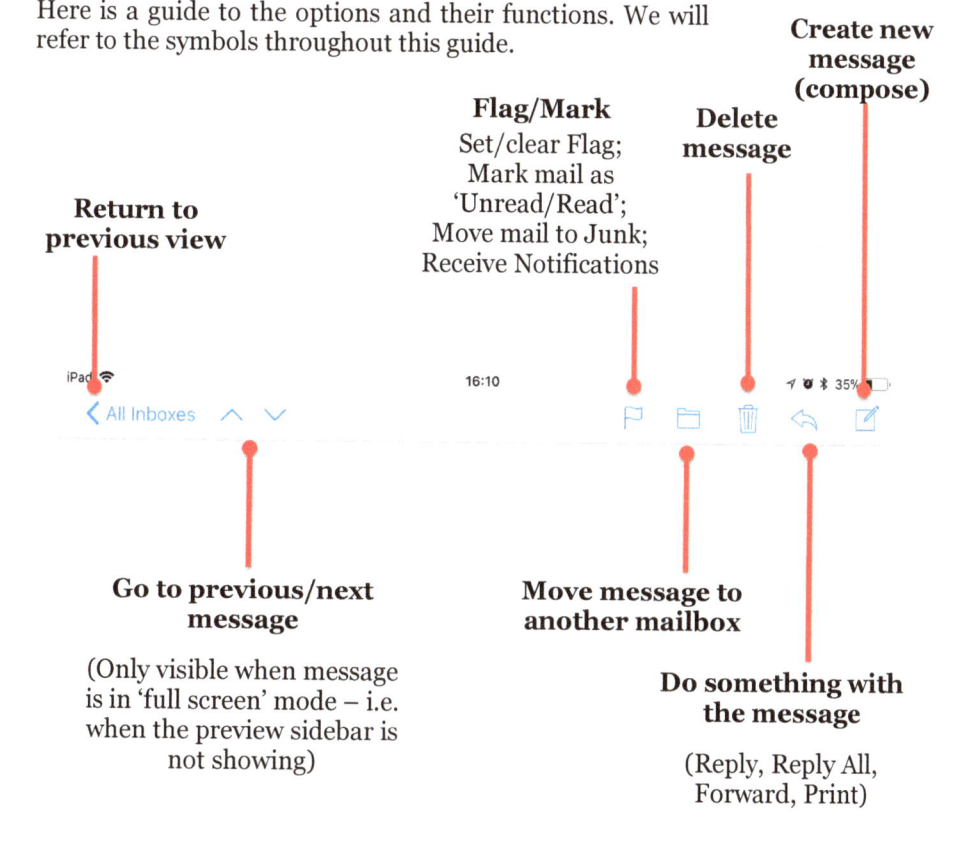

Create new message (compose)

Flag/Mark
Set/clear Flag;
Mark mail as
'Unread/Read';
Move mail to Junk;
Receive Notifications

Delete message

Return to previous view

Go to previous/next message

(Only visible when message is in 'full screen' mode – i.e. when the preview sidebar is not showing)

Move message to another mailbox

Do something with the message

(Reply, Reply All, Forward, Print)

Receiving and Reading your Mail

How do I see what mail I have received?

You will often see a 'badge' (a number in a round circle) on the Mail app on your Home screen. This badge tells you how many mail messages are yet to be read.

You may also hear a sound and receive a notification that a new email has arrived. (This is determined in Notifications – something covered in iTandCoffee's guide **A Guided Tour of the iPad & iPhone**.)

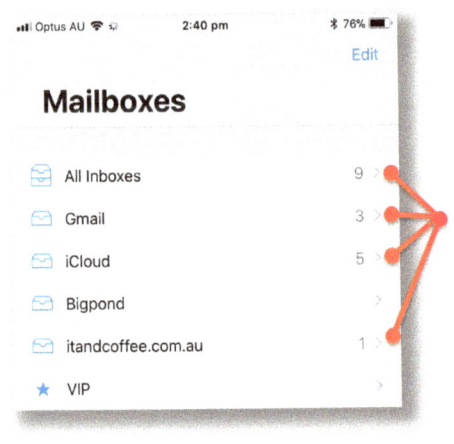

Touch on your **Mail** app on **the Home screen** to open the app.

You will find all your 'incoming' mail in your **Inbox** (one of your Mailboxes, as described in the previous section).

A number beside the Inbox (or any of your other Mailboxes) shows the number of 'unread' mail messages to be found in that mailbox.

If you have multiple accounts, touch on **All Inboxes** to see all incoming mail, or touch on the name of your mail account under All Inboxes to just view that account's incoming mail.

The preview list

Once you choose a mailbox (on right is my Gmail Inbox on my iPhone), you will then be shown a preview list of the mailbox's contents.

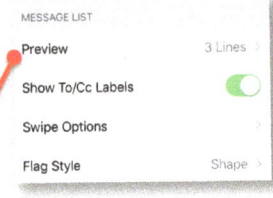

The number of lines that you see for each message in the preview list will depend on your **Settings -> Mail -> Preview**.

In the example on the right, I have chosen to show 3 preview lines; on the next page, the image shows my preview list on the iPad with 2 preview lines.

Receiving and Reading your Mail

On the iPad in 'Landscape' orientation, the preview list will be on the left permanently (as shown below).

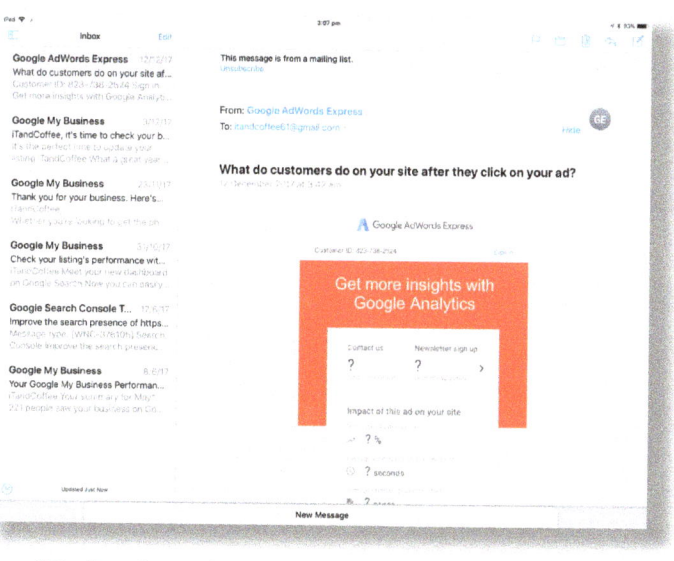

On an iPad in 'Portrait' orientation (see right), the preview sidebar will disappear when you tap on a message in the list, or when you tap on the full message on the right side.

This preview sidebar will come back when you

- drag it back into to view by swiping from the left edge of the screen towards the right or

- tap < at top left.

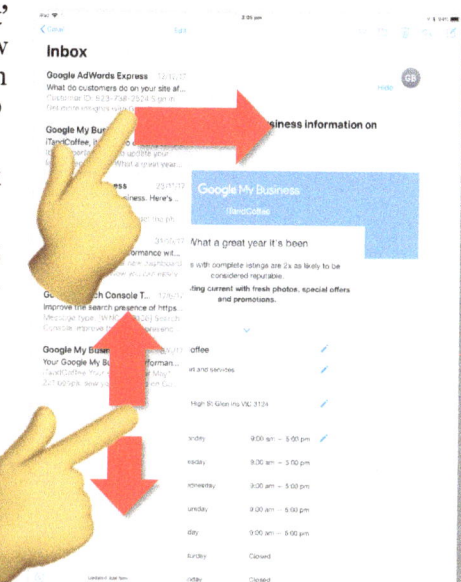

If you are on iPhone, the preview list will fill the entire the screen (as shown in the example on the previous page).

If you don't see the list of emails on your iPhone, you may be in an individual email – so choose < at top left to 'go back' to your list of messages.

On both iPad and iPhone, drag up and down on the sidebar list to navigate and view the list of emails in your Mailbox.

Receiving and Reading your Mail

View the content of an email

In the preview list, just tap anywhere on the email that you would like to view.

The message that you tap will be shaded grey and will appear in full on the right (or fill your screen if you are on an iPhone or have your iPad in 'Portrait' orientation).

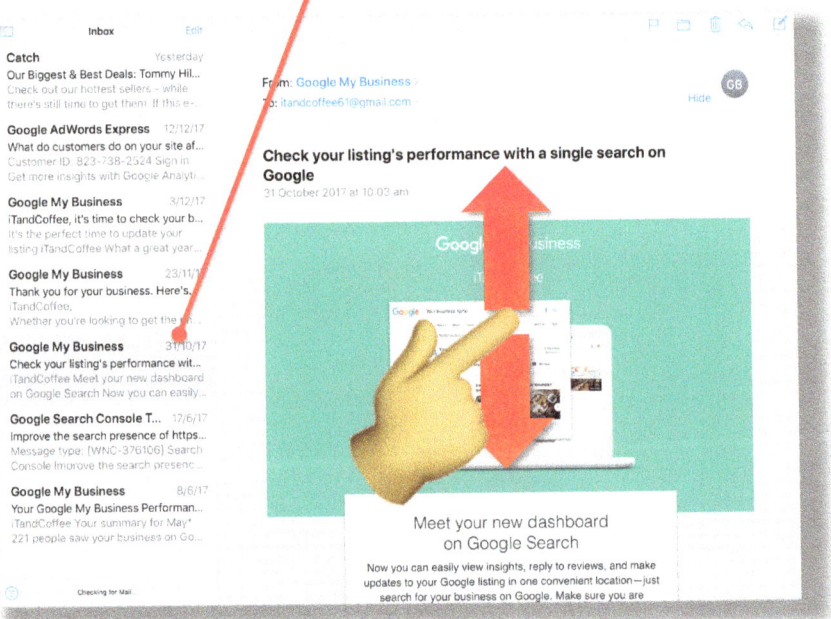

Drag up and down on the displayed message to view the parts of the message that are not in view.

The message will remain the selected email for this mailbox until you select a different message. So, if you exit mail, then come back in later, the same message will appear as the 'currently selected' message.

Just touch on another message in the preview list to replace it with another. If you do not see your preview list, tap < at top left to get it back.

What order are my emails in the preview list

Your emails are shown in descending date/time order, with your most recently received emails always at the 'top' of the list.

If you are not seeing your latest emails – for example those that have arrived today - you may need to swipe down on the list (perhaps repeatedly) to see those emails that are 'higher up' in list.

Receiving and Reading your Mail

Identifying new emails

Any unread emails are highlighted with a blue dot on left.

● **Spotify**   16/12/17
Act now! $11.99 for 3 months of Premium.
Be unstoppable in 2018. Go Premium to play all of the
music you love non-stop, ad-free. Just $11.99 for 3 m...

Once you have touched on an email to read it, this dot will disappear.

How do I 'close' an email once I have read it?

This is something I get asked a lot, especially by people using an iPad.

When you have finished reading an email on your iPad but don't yet want to delete it, how do you 'get out of it' – how do you 'close' it so that it is no longer showing on the main part of the screen.

Well, the short answer is that you don't really. Your iPad is not like your PC, where you press an 'x' to make the message disappear.

If you don't want the message any more, you delete it by tapping the Trash symbol.

If you don't want to delete it at this point, simply choose another message to view instead.

If you are on an iPhone, or on an iPad in Portrait mode, you can also use the 'up and down arrow' symbols ∧ ∨ to move to the next or previous message in the mailbox.

On your iPhone, just choose < to return to your preview list, where you can choose a different email from the list.

Receiving and Reading your Mail

Marking a message as 'Unread'

If you decide that you would like the email message to appear as 'unread' again (perhaps to remind you to come back to it later), tap the 'Flag' symbol that will appear at bottom left on the iPhone, or top right on the iPad and choose the option **Mark as Unread**.

Alternatively, **slide from left to right** on the message in the preview list and tap **Unread.**

The blue dot will re-appear.

If the email is currently 'Unread', the option that that shows when you swipe left to right on the preview list item will be 'Read' – i.e. mark the message as 'Read'.

If you see some other option than this when you swipe a preview item from left to right, it may be that a standard setting has been changed.

Go to **Settings -> Mail -> Swipe Options** and tap **Swipe Right** to choose an alternate option for this action (i.e. None, Flag or Archive).

Retrieving mail manually – for when you can't wait!

Your mail is typically retrieved from your mail provider on a regular basis – but this might only be every 15 minutes.

The frequency with which your email is checked and downloaded will depend on settings in **Settings -> Accounts and Passwords -> Fetch New Data**. (We'll cover this in more detail later)

So, what do you do if you are waiting on an urgent email that you know someone has just sent to you, but that hasn't arrived yet?

Receiving and Reading your Mail

You can do a manual 'refresh' at any time to retrieve the latest mail from your mail provider. Just **drag down** (i.e. touch your finger to the upper part of the preview sidebar, drag down and let go).

The 'refresh' symbol 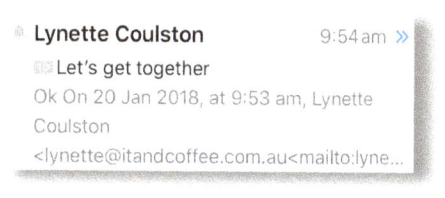 will appear (as indicated with the red circle in the previous image), and your latest mail will be downloaded and displayed at the top of the preview list.

Grouped emails – 'Threads'

Do you ever find that you have several emails grouped together, and showing a double-arrow » on the right of the message's day/time?

> **Lynette Coulston** 9:54 am »
> ✉ Let's get together
> Ok On 20 Jan 2018, at 9:53 am, Lynette Coulston
> <lynette@itandcoffee.com.au<mailto:lyne...

If you see the symbol on the right of the date/time of an item in the preview list,
it means that your mail is being 'grouped by thread'.

A thread is a set of emails that were to or from one or more recipients, about the same subject.

Only the latest message in the conversation/thread is shown in the preview sidebar.

If your device is set up to do such grouping by thread, an email you are looking for may be 'hidden' in one of these groups, making it harder to locate – since it will not then appear in the full preview list on the date/time that it was received.

This grouping is determined by a Mail Setting.

To enable or stop such grouping, go to **Settings-> Mail** and turn on/off **Organise by Thread**.

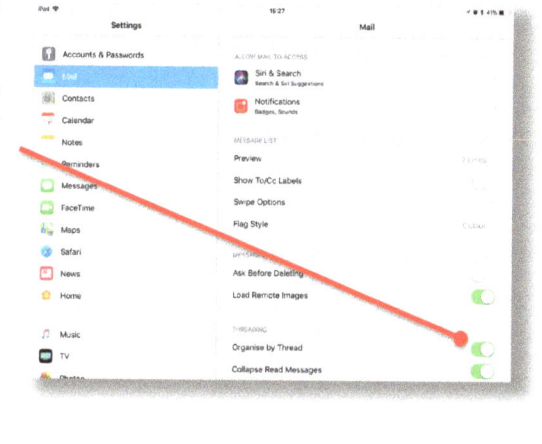

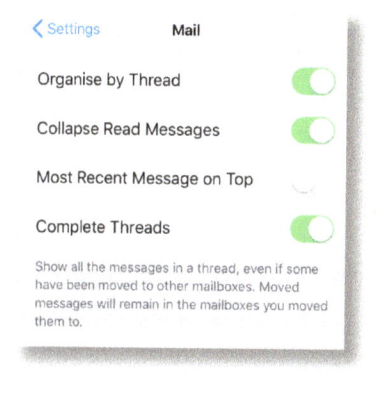

25

Receiving and Reading your Mail

If you do like organising your mail in this way, you can 'expand' the thread and view previews of all » of the thread's mail messages by tapping on the double-arrow symbol.

The arrows change to point downwards ⌄ , and the list of messages in the thread are shown. In the example on the right, there are 2.

Tap any of these messages to view that part of the conversation. Or tap on the top message in the thread to view all of the messages.

Tap ⌄ again to summarise the thread again (and hide all but the latest message in the thread). The symbol will change back to »

You also have several other options in your Mail Settings if you choose to **Organise by Thread.**

These settings relate to what appears when you tap on any message that has a 'thread' of other messages associated with it – what level of detail is shown in the 'full screen' mode for the message/s.

Collapse Read Messages will only show a summary line for any message in the Thread that you have already read.

If you want the latest message to appear first, turn on **Most Recent Messages on Top.**

If **Complete Threads** is turned on, you will see ALL messages that are part of the same conversation whether they are in your Sent mailbox, Deleted mailbox or any other mailbox.

In the example on the right, the latest message in this thread is on the top, and with my most recent reply (from my Sent mail) shown below that.

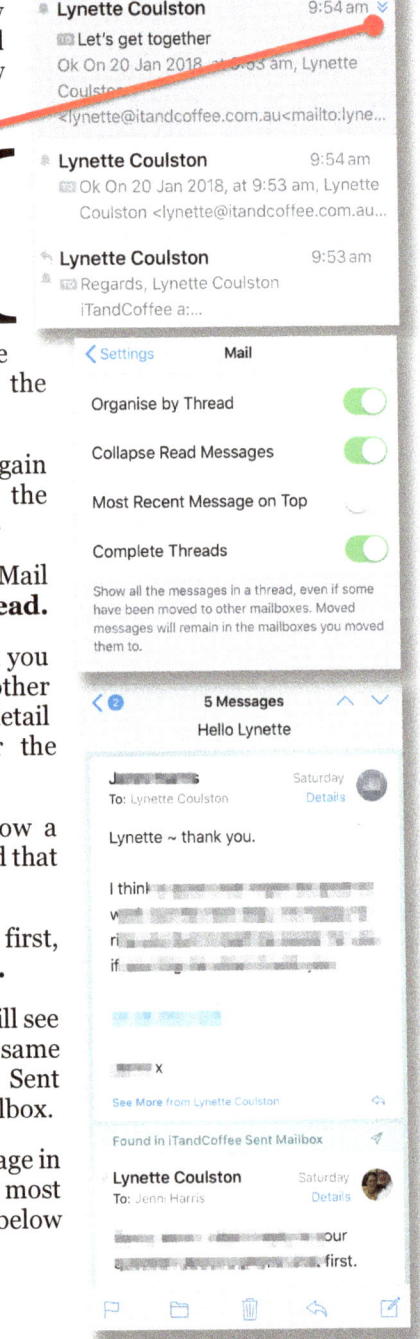

Creating and Sending Mail

Compose your email

Create a new email by selecting the 'compose email' symbol, which is top right on iPad and bottom right on iPhone.

There are three basic things that you will need to enter when you create an email:

- o The **recipient** in the 'To' field.
- o The **subject** in the '**Subject**' field.
- o The **message** body – in the area underneath Subject.

First things first - address your mail message

First, enter the intended recipient of the email in the 'To' field. You can do this by typing the email address OR the name of one of your Contacts.

When you start typing, a list of any matching names and email addresses may drop down below the 'To' field (if any exist in your device).

This list will show any matches from your **Contacts** (i.e. your address book on your device) for what you have typed – Contacts that have an email address recorded against them.

Your device also 'remembers' any name and email addresses that have been seen previously in Mail messages, so a few letters may be enough to identify the recipient.

If you see the person/email address you need in the pop-down list, just touch on it to select it – and you will see it added to your '**To**' field.

Creating and Sending Mail

Don't worry if you then see the name of the person (or business) shown in the 'To' field, instead of the email address. Your device knows the email address that goes with the name - as long as it is stored in your Contacts or you have had previous 'correspondence' with the person.

To: Jim Coulston, | ⊕

If you are entering an email address in full (rather than selecting an existing Contact), make sure your email address doesn't have spaces in it and it has a format like **name@isp.com.** Select **return** on the keyboard when you have finished entry of the email address and the entered email address will turn blue.

If the 'contact' or email address you have entered is blue, you can choose another recipient by following the same steps. Choose as many recipients for the email as you need.

Another way to select your recipients is to touch on the blue ⊕ sign that you will see on the right when you have touched on the **To** field.

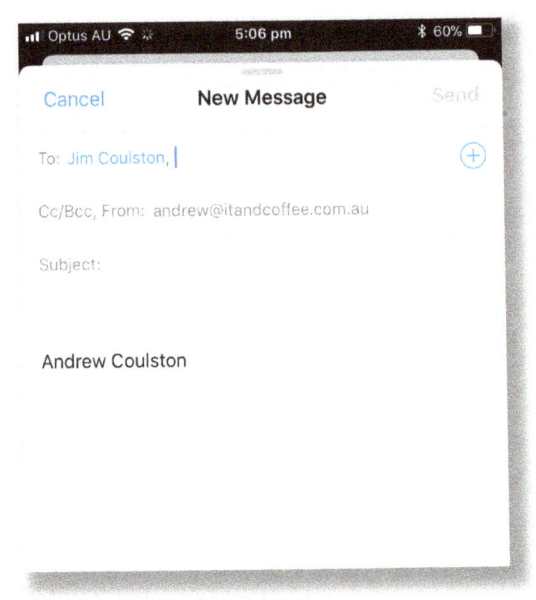

This will show your **Contacts** list, allowing you to search for and choose (by tapping) a name from this list

That name will then appear in the 'To' field.

Only Contacts that have an email address recorded will be able to be selected.

Creating and Sending Mail

Enter your Subject

Touch the subject field to position your cursor on that field.

This is where you describe the topic of your email. You can leave this out if you like, but you will get a warning when you choose 'Send' if you have left it out (which you can choose to ignore).

(You will notice in the image on the right that the heading bar of your email will update to reflect your email's subject!)

Now it's time to get writing!!

Touch your finger at the top of the body of the email (just below the Subject field), then type in the text of your email. It can be as long or short as you like! The sentences will automatically 'wrap' onto the next line as you keep typing.

To add new lines to your email and include spacing between paragraphs, just select the **return** key on your keyboard – this will 'push down' any email signature you may already have in the email and provide more space for you to type.

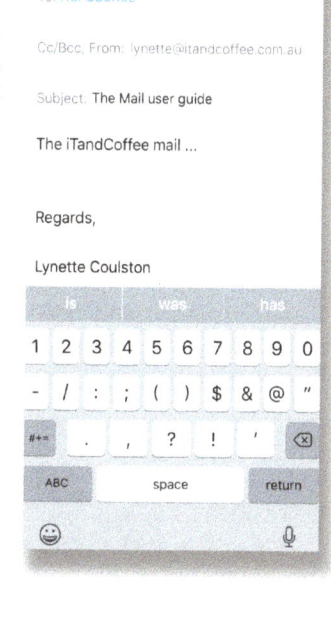

Why is there text already in the email's body?

You may already see some text in the body of the email – perhaps it shows 'Sent from my iPad' or 'Sent from my iPhone'.

This is called your email **Signature**, and can be customised to show something other than this in your Mail **Settings** - at **Settings -> Mail -> Signature**

Just tap in the signature box to compose your signature (and remove the default if you don't want it).

If you have more than one email account, you can choose to set up a single email signature for **All Accounts** or tap **Per Account** to set up different signatures for each.

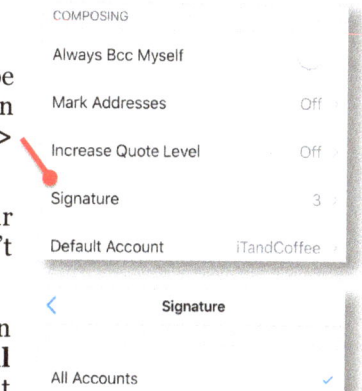

Creating and Sending Mail

Sign-off and send

Once you have finished drafting your email, you can sign off, and then select **Send**.

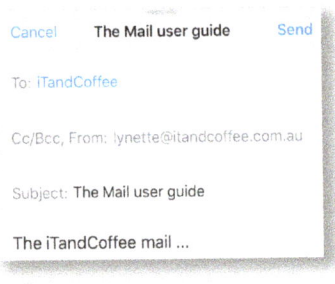

Of course, you must be connected to the Internet via mobile data or Wi-Fi for the email to be successfully sent.

Don't be fooled by the whoosh

Don't be fooled by the **whoosh** sound that you might hear, the one that makes it sounds like the email was sent immediately!

If you are not currently connected to the Internet, the email will go into a temporary Mailbox called the **Outbox**.

Once you are connected again to the internet, it should automatically send. If you ever see an Outbox in your list of Mailboxes, it means that you probably have one or more emails that haven't yet sent.

For some email accounts, an email that is sent when you are away from home will not send until you get back home and on your home Internet connection.

Have you encountered this problem when away from home? Make an appointment with iTandCoffee to talk about how to solve this, if you are finding it is causing you grief.

But what if I'm not yet ready to send?

If you are not quite ready to send and want to instead save this email for sending later, select **Cancel** (top left), then **Save Draft.**

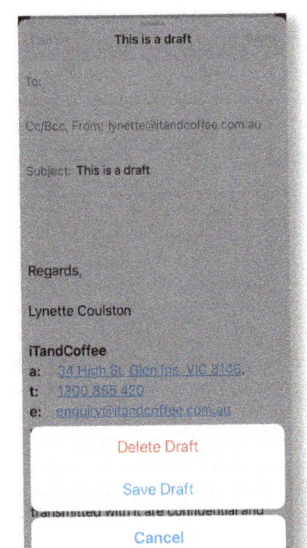

You will be able to go to your **Drafts** folder later, open the email and send it.

Of course, if you don't want to keep the email you just started, just choose **Delete Draft**.

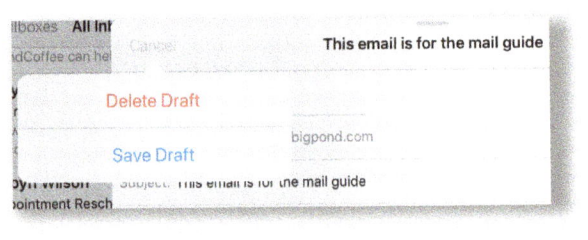

Creating and Sending Mail

If, whilst working on an email, you wish to look at other emails or your other mailboxes, simply tap the bar at the top of the email and drag it all the way to the bottom of ⸻ the screen.

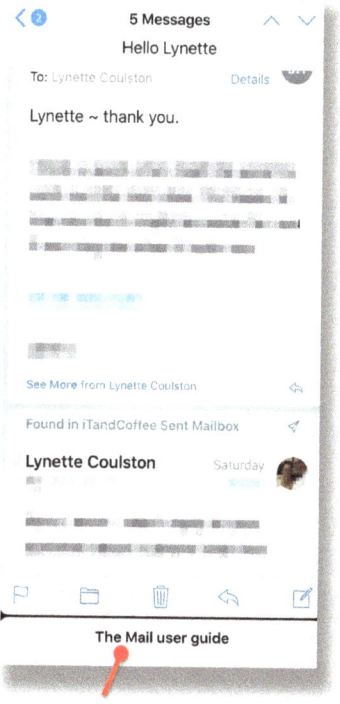

The message will sit as a bar at the bottom of the screen until you tap on the bar to open that draft email again.

If you have 'dragged down' several emails, tapping on the bar at the bottom of the screen will show a screen that lists all the drafts that have been dragged out of the way.

Tap any of these emails to continue drafting and sending.

If you don't need to keep any one (or more) of these emails, swipe them off to the left to delete them.

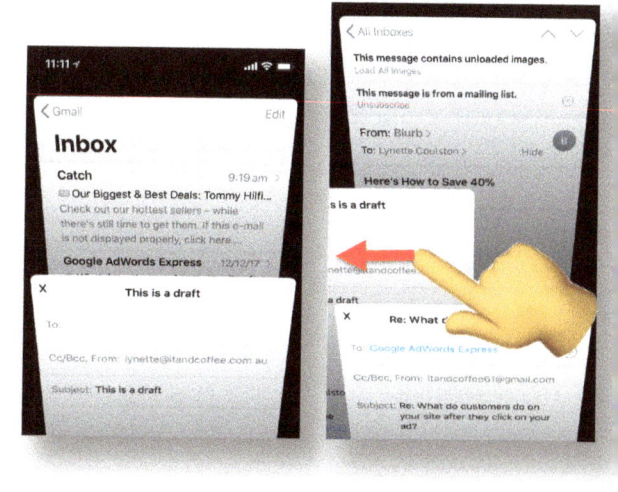

Creating and Sending Mail

Quickly get to your saved draft emails!

If you have chosen to save any draft emails (rather than dragging them to the bottom of the screen), these emails can be found in the **Drafts** Mailbox.

But there is a quicker way to check your list of Draft emails.

Hold your finger on the 'Compose' icon  until the list of draft emails appear.

From this list, touch on the Draft email that you want to open and continue writing it and/or send it.

Other fields you will see in your email

There are three additional fields that you can fill in when creating an email. Normally, these fields are grouped together. If you touch on the **Cc/Bcc** words, (or **Cc/Bcc, From** for some people) you will see the list of fields expand to show separate entry fields for **Cc**, **Bcc** and (sometimes) **From**.

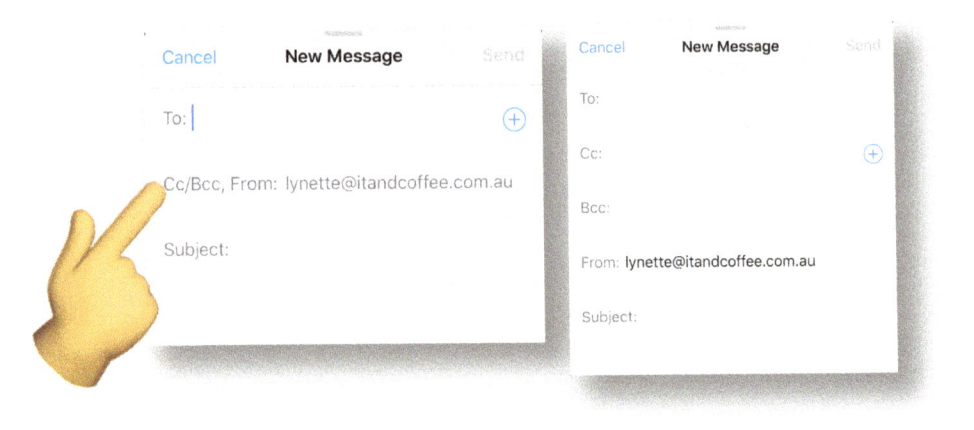

Let's look at the meaning and use of these additional fields.

Creating and Sending Mail

The 'Cc' field

Cc stands for Courtesy Copy, which means that you are 'copying' a person in on this email so that they know about it, but that it is not for their direct attention and action.

Touch on the **Cc/Bcc** field if you would like to 'Cc' someone on your email, and then touch on the **Cc** field to position the cursor there

Enter the applicable person's name or email address in the **Cc** field – same as for the 'To' field.

When the email is sent, the 'Cc'd' person will receive it, but they will see that they are on the **Cc** list only.

It is important to note that everyone who gets the email can see who is on the 'To' and 'Cc' list and has access to those people's email address details.

But what do you do when you want to send an email to lots of people, but don't want them to see each other's names and email addresses? That is where **Bcc** comes in.

The 'Bcc' field

Bcc stands for Blind Courtesy Copy.

When you include names in the **Bcc** field, the recipients listed in the **Bcc** field will not be visible to anyone who receives the email - only the **To** and **Cc** list of names/addresses will be visible (if there are any).

Touch on **Cc/Bcc** to 'expose' the **Bcc** field and enter applicable contact/email address.

This is the field that you should use whenever you are sending emails to a long list of recipients.

Note that anyone **Bcc**'d who chooses to Reply All (described shortly) will only be sending their reply to the **To** and **Cc** list – but not to the **Bcc** list.

Creating and Sending Mail

The 'From' field *(only for those with multiple email accounts)*

This field only appears if you have more than one email account on the device. It allows you to choose the email address from which to send the email.

The **From** address for each email is automatically filled in for you but can be changed if ever you need to send from a different email address.

For example, you may need to do this in the case where an email won't send when you are away from your home internet.

Just touch on the **From** field to see a list of your available email addresses.

Touch on the email address that you wish to use in this case, and the **From** field will be filled in to reflect your selection.

Choosing which email address is your Default

For those who have multiple email addresses, the **From** email address that appears when a new email is 'composed' will depend on what mailbox you were in when you created the email, and on the 'default email address' that you have selected in your Mail Settings.

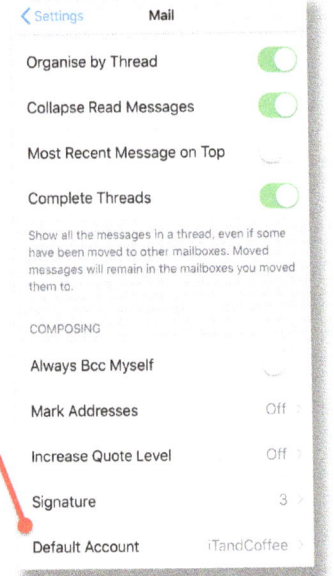

If you are in your 'All Inboxes', the default email address from **Settings** will be used.

If you are in a specific account's mailbox, the email address that appears in **From** will be that account's email address.

To change your default email address that is use from All Inboxes and from other Apps, go to **Settings -> Mail -> Default Account** and select the required 'default' email address from the list.

Creating and Sending Mail

Set a Notification on an email

There may be times when you will send an email and want to get a special notification of any responses – and then track those responses.

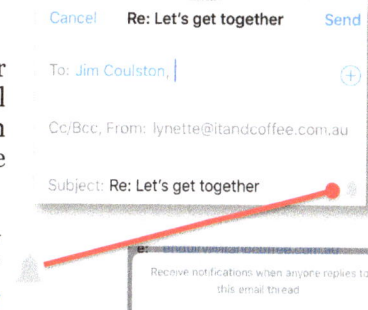

While you may be used to getting a sound for any email that is received, setting a special notification on an email can really help when you are awaiting response/s that are particularly important.

To receive special notifications about any responses to your email, simply tap on the 'bell' symbol in the subject field and choose **Notify Me**

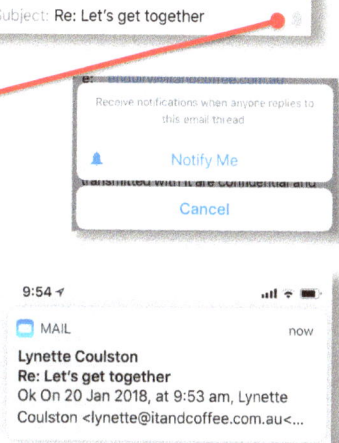

The bell symbol will turn blue.

Then, when any reply is received for that email, you see a special notification appear on your screen, highlighting that there has been a response.

You will also be able to view all such responses in the **Thread Notifications** smart album (in Mailboxes).

Replying to and Forwarding Emails

To reply to an email, or forward an email to someone else, select the **Reply** option from top right of the screen (on iPad) or the bottom of the screen (on iPhone).

Choose from the options shown

- **Reply** to reply to sender only.
- **Reply All** to reply to sender and all people in the 'To' and 'Cc' list (and excluding the 'Bcc' list). This option is only available if the email was sent to more than one person, either in the To or Cc field.
- **Forward** to forward the email to someone else.

When you choose any of these three options, a new email is created for you with the '**Subject**' field already filled in. The letters **Re:** will be added to the front of subject for **Reply** and **Reply All**, while **Fwd:** will be added for Forward.

Reply

For the **Reply** options, the **To** field will be automatically filled in and the cursor will be positioned at the top of the body of the email, ready for you to type your reply.

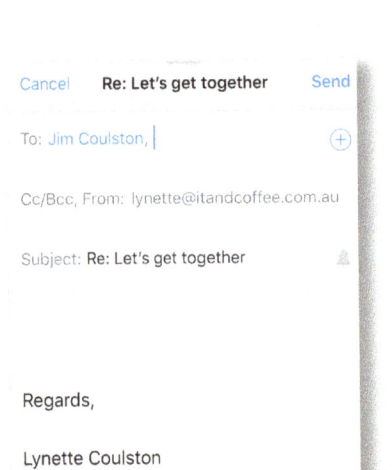

Reply All

For the **Reply All** option, the **To** field will be filled in with the sender's email address, and the **Cc** field will have the email addresses of all other recipients of the original email (whether they were in the **To** or **Cc** field). As for Reply, the cursor will be positioned at the top of the body of the email, ready for you to type.

Forward

For the **Forward** option, your cursor will be positioned at the **To** field, ready for you to choose the recipient/s of the forwarded email. Once you have done this, if you wish to add a message to the forwarded message, tap at the top of the body of the message to set the cursor position, and type your message.

Once you have completed filling in any required information, tap **Send**.

Deleting Emails

Cleaning up – how do I delete emails?

It's a good idea to keep your Inbox (and even your Sent) mailbox under control by deleting emails that you no longer need. Emails can be deleted individually, or in 'bulk'.

Before we go into talking about methods of deleting emails, let's just make sure that you can see the 'bin' symbol that we will be referring to.

If you don't see a bin symbol – but instead see a 'box' symbol, this means that your Mail account has been set up to 'archive' your mail instead of deleting it. Jump to the end of this section to find out how to change your settings the get the 'bin' instead.

Method 1 - Deleting an individual email after viewing it.

Touch on the email that you want to delete so that you see it on the right-hand side or in 'full screen'.

Select the **Bin** symbol

- From the bottom of the email on the iPhone.
- From the top of the email on the iPad.

Your email will be 'jump into' the **Bin** mailbox.

A warning if you have turned on 'Organise by Thread'

If your emails are 'grouped by thread' (so that they appear in the preview sidebar with » on the right – as shown below), the number of emails in the thread will be shown at the top of the main message screen when you tap on the item in the preview list.

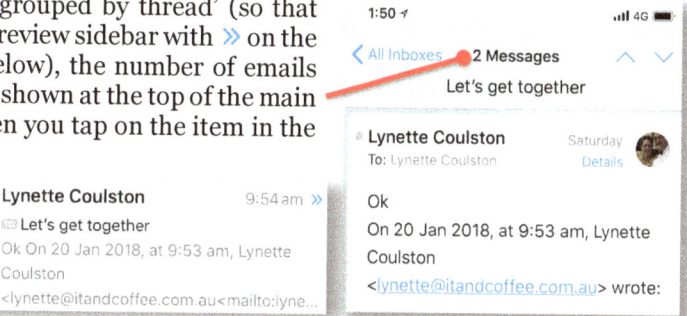

Deleting Emails

In this case, choosing the Bin symbol will delete **all** messages in that thread. For the example below, 2 messages will be deleted.

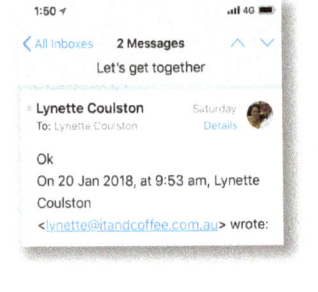

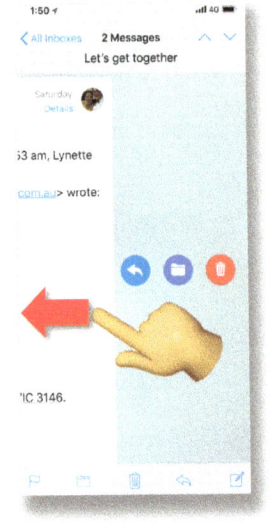

If you don't wish to delete all messages in a 'thread', you must choose which item of the thread to delete.

This is done by swiping the individual message in the thread to the left.

This will uncover three options, including the bin option. Tap this bin to delete the individual message (instead of the entire 'thread').

Method 2 - Deleting an individual email from the preview list

From the preview list (where you see the summarised list of your emails), swipe right to left on the email to delete it.

Swiping all the way to the left edge will immediately delete the message.

Swiping part way across the preview list will show three options – **More**, **Flag** and **Bin**. Tap the **Bin** icon to delete the message.

A warning again about Threads

If there is a number appearing under the bin symbol, you will be deleting that number of emails.

As mentioned above, this scenario occurs when you have several messages grouped as a 'Thread'.

Touch on the **Bin** icon to delete ALL the emails in the Thread

If you don't intend on deleted all of the emails in the thread, see Method 1 (above) for how to delete individual emails in the thread.

Deleting Emails

Method 3 - Deleting several emails at once

Go to the mailbox that contains the emails to be deleted.

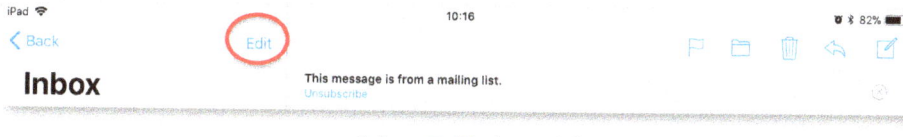

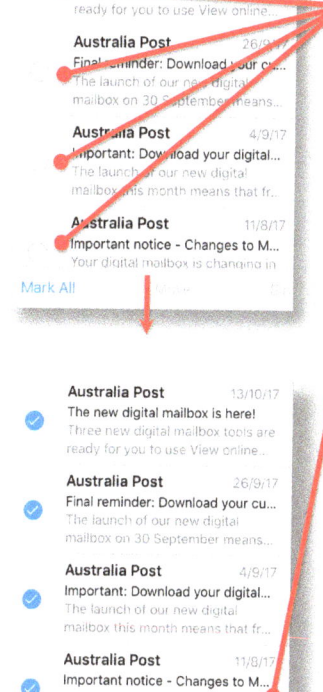

Select **Edit** (top right of email list). The emails will be listed with a circle on the left.

Touch on the circle next to each of the emails that you want to delete – a 'tick' will show.

The number that you have selected will show in the heading above the list.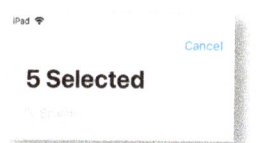

Choose the **Bin** option (bottom right of the preview list) to complete the deletion process and sent the selected emails to the Bin mailbox.

Oh No! I deleted the wrong email!

Fear not – deleted emails can be recovered and put back where they belong!

Go to the **Bin** mailbox (or to the **'All Rubbish'** consolidated mailbox for those who have multiple email accounts).

Select the email that you need to recover, then choose the symbol ☐ (move mailboxes/refile) from the toolbar (top on iPad, bottom on iPhone).

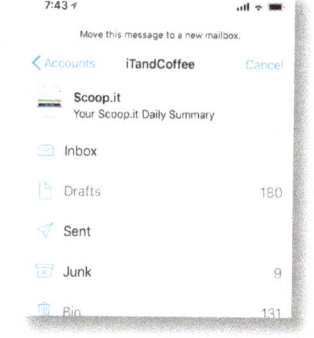

As screen will appear with the heading **Move this message to a new mailbox**.

From the list mailboxes that you are shown, tap on the mailbox to which you want to return the deleted email – which is usually your Inbox.

Deleting Emails

There is also a quicker, nifty trick for undoing an action such as accidental deletion of an email.

Shake your device to undo!

Yes, that's right – shake your device. Be careful not to drop your heavier iPad in the process!

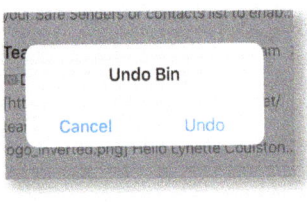

This will bring up a confirmation window - tap Undo to reverse the deletion!

The **Shake to Undo** setting can be enabled/disabled from **Settings -> General -> Accessibility**, under the INTERACTION heading.

How long do deleted emails stay on my iPhone iPad?

For your email account's deleted emails, you can usually specify how long to retain the emails that have been moved to the Bin – meaning they can be automatically deleted permanently after a nominated period of time.

For some accounts like Gmail, Hotmail and Yahoo, you must log into your account using a web browser and adjust the permanent deletion settings from there.

For some accounts, this can be done on the iPad or iPhone, from **Settings > Accounts & Passwords**.

Adjusting iCloud Deletion Settings

Let's look at **iCloud email accounts** first, as the steps are just a bit different to other accounts.

1. Tap on your iCloud Account in **Settings -> Accounts & Passwords.**

2. Swipe to the **bottom** of the screen to see the **Mail** option under the **ADVANCED** heading. Tap **Mail.**

3. At the bottom of the next screen (under the 'Outgoing Mail Server' setting) tap **Advanced**.

Deleting Emails

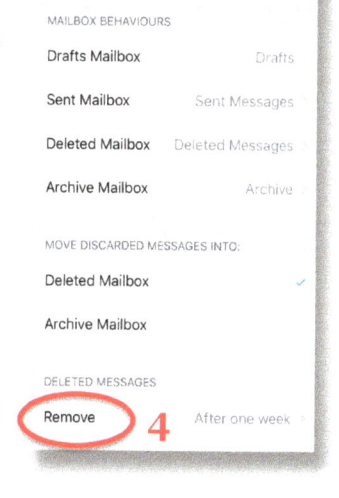

4. Tap **Remove** under DELETED MESSAGES.

5. Choose how long to keep messages (i.e. when should they be removed permanently).

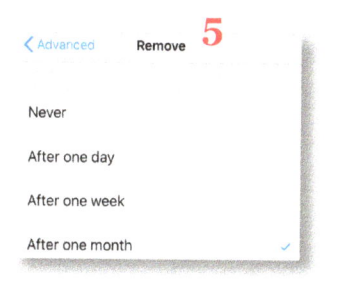

6. Now save your changes – Choose <Advanced (see 5 above), then choose < again to return to the previous screen.

Choose Done at top right of that screen to complete the changes to your iCloud account settings.

Adjusting Other Account Deletion Settings

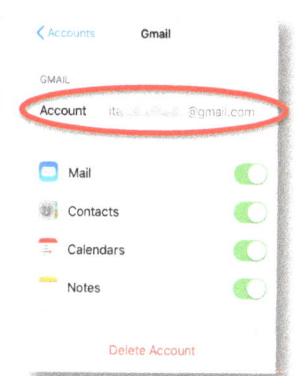

It is probably worth checking if you can adjust the email deletion settings from your iPad/iPhone before visiting the webmail settings.

Tap on your account name in **Settings -> Accounts & Passwords**, then tap on your email address at the top.

As for iCloud accounts, choose the **Advanced** option that you see at the bottom of that screen, then look for the same **Remove** under DELETED MESSAGES (see above for more details).

But I see a box ⬜ instead of a bin! 🗑

If you see a 'box' symbol where you should see the 'bin', this means that your mail account has been set to 'archive' your messages instead of 'binning' them. This is frustrating, because they are never deleted – instead going to the Archive Mailbox.

This generally occurs for Gmail account users. We'll look at how to adjust Gmail (and other IMAP) account settings shortly. Firstly, we'll look at iCloud.

Deleting Emails

For iCloud

For your **iCloud** email account, follow steps 1-3 as described earlier in this section, to get to the **Advanced** set of options for your iCloud mail account.

Look for the MOVE DISCARDED MESSAGES INTO section.

If the **Archive Mailbox** option is ticked, then tap the **Deleted Mailbox** option instead.

Choose <, then Done to complete the change.

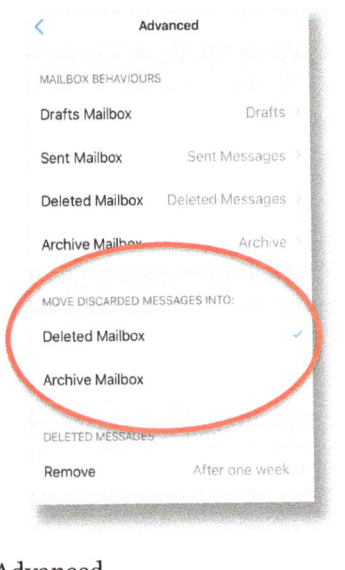

For Gmail, Hotmail, Yahoo and other IMAP/Exchange accounts

Tap on your Gmail account in **Settings -> Accounts & Passwords**

Tap on your email address at the top, then choose Advanced.

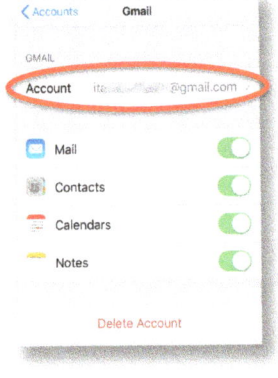
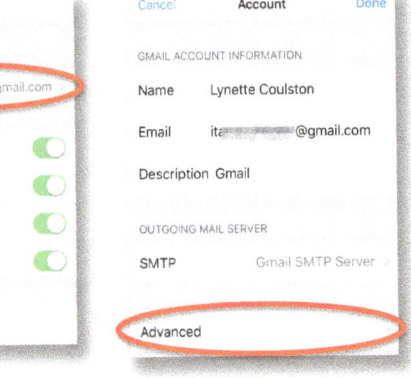
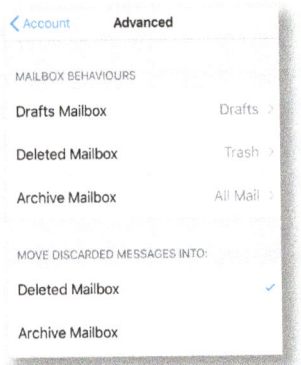

If the **Archive Mailbox** option is ticked under MOVE DISCARDED MESSAGES INTO, then tap the **Deleted Mailbox** option instead.

Choose <, then Done to complete the change.

Printing Emails

To print an email that you are viewing, select and choose the '**Print**' option from the list of options provided.

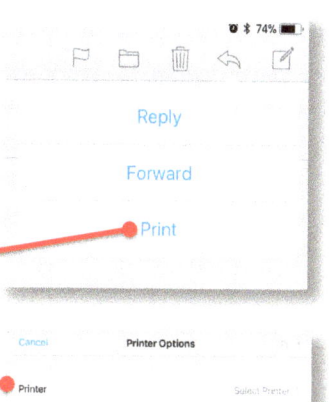

You will need to have a Wi-Fi printer that supports a feature called **Airprint**. Not all printers have this capability.

If you are not sure if your Wi-Fi printer supports printing from your iPad or iPhone, why not just try selecting the **Print** option.

Touch on **Select Printer**.

You will be presented with a list of available printers – but only if your iPad/iPhone can detect any on your Wi-Fi network.

If you see your printer listed, just touch on it to select it.

Then touch on Print to print the email.

Before you print, you can adjust the number of copies (by pressing +/-)

You may also see **Options,** giving access to choose from available printing options for that printer. Below is the set that I see for my Epson printer.

If your printer is a Wi-Fi printer with Airprint capability, make sure that it is connected to your Wi-Fi network.

Then, make sure that your iPad or iPhone is also connected to that same Wi-Fi network.

To find out if your printer has the 'Airprint' capability, refer to the web Apple Support website, at http://support.apple.com/kb/HT4356.

Finding Your Mail

Finding Sent Mail

Emails that you send are stored in the **Sent** Mailbox of your email account.

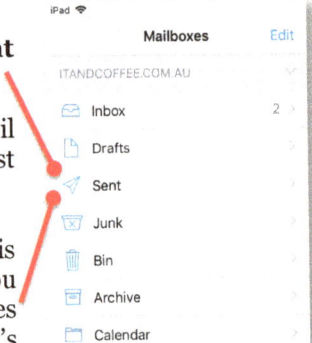

Touch on this Mailbox to see your sent mail sorted in reverse date/time order - i.e. your last sent email is first in the list.

If you have more than one email account, there is one **Sent** mailbox per mail account, which you can view by **1.** Scrolling through your mailboxes until you reach the applicable account's subsection and then **2.** touching on Sent.

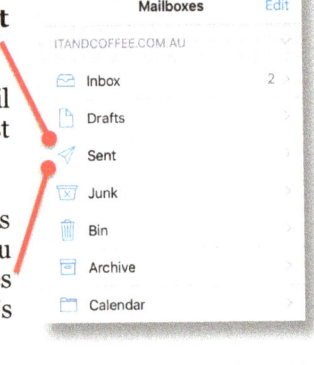

You can also see your Sent mail in the special 'smart' mailbox, **'All Sent'** (if you enabled this 'smart mailbox' – see the earlier description on how to do this.)

I can't find an email sent from my computer?

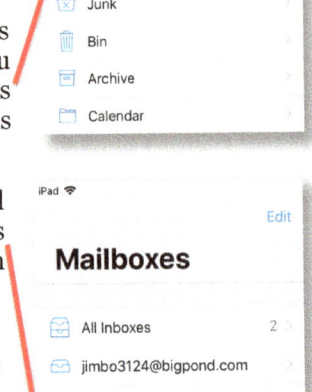

Emails that you sent from your iPhone may not be able to be viewed from another mobile device or your computer, and vice-versa.

This depends on what type of email account you have, and how it is installed in each instance.

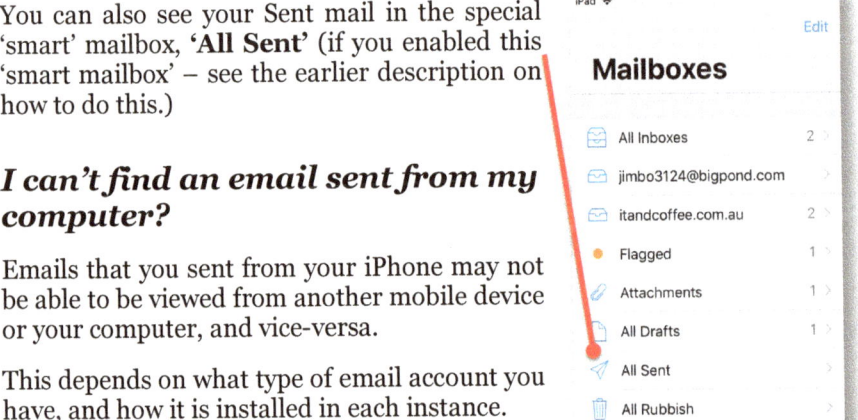

For some types of accounts – known as Pop email accounts - the Sent mail may only be stored on the device from which it was sent, and not 'synchronised' to any other computer or device.

This means you may need to search more than one device for an email that you sent.

Pop email accounts download copies of your emails to your devices and you are then working with these copies, not a 'central' version of the emails.

Other types of account - such as Gmail, Hotmail/Outlook, Yahoo, iCloud and Exchange - allow you to view all your sent mail, regardless of which device you sent the message from. You are working with a 'centrally stored' view of your mail that updates regularly. These are known as IMAP mail accounts.

You will find more on the different types of mail accounts towards the end of this section.

Finding Your Mail

Searching using a search phrase

It can sometimes be difficult to find an email that you are looking for, especially if your Inbox gets a bit too full!

Your Mail app provides the ability to 'Search' for a mail message, by simply entering a few letters of a contact's name or email address, or perhaps the subject of the message.

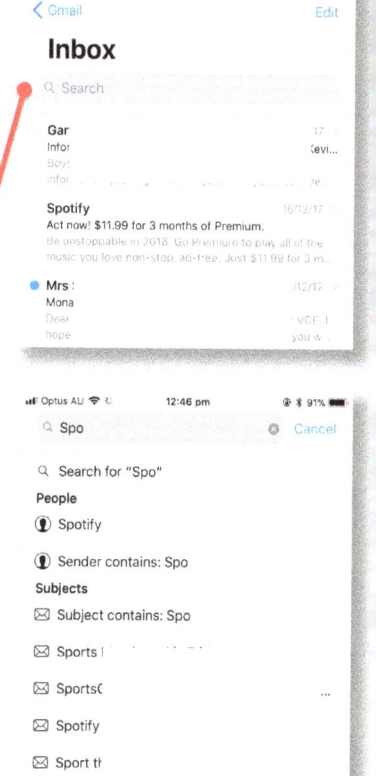

The **Search** field is available when you are looking at your preview list of emails, sometimes hidden above the first email in the list.

To reveal the **Search** field, drag down on the message list.

Just type in some letters, and a list of matched suggestions will appear – for **People** and **Subjects** that match.

Touch on any item in this list to view all emails that fit the criteria or tap on any listed individual email to view that message.

Select Cancel to clear the search field and return to viewing all the mail in the mailbox.

Choosing where to search

A feature introduced in more recent iOS versions is the ability to choose whether to search in just the Current Mailbox, or in All Mailboxes.

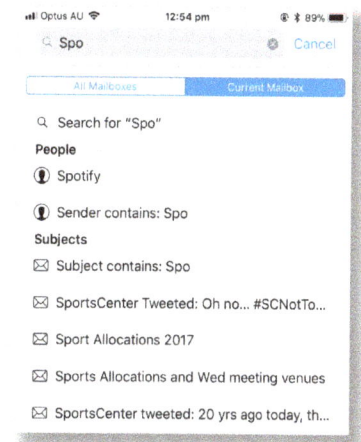

If you don't see these options below the search bar, just 'pull down' the list of search results to uncover them.

Tap either of these options to see more or less suggested matches.

Finding Your Mail

Filtering mail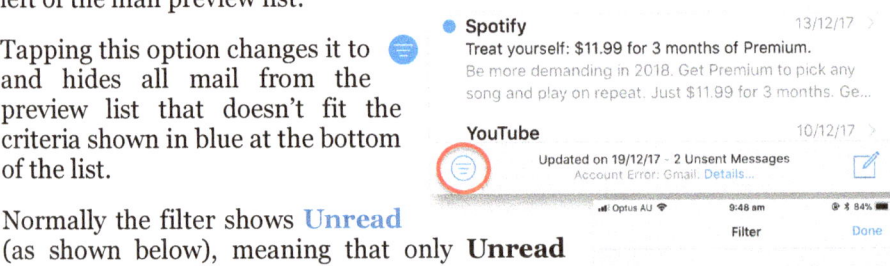

In addition to the ability to directly search and seek out specific emails, the Mail app comes with easy access to a 'Filter' option, which is located at the bottom left of the mail preview list.

Tapping this option changes it to and hides all mail from the preview list that doesn't fit the criteria shown in blue at the bottom of the list.

Normally the filter shows Unread (as shown below), meaning that only **Unread** emails appear when the filter is on.

Filtered by:
Unread

Tapping the words **Filtered by:** brings up the **Filter** menu (shown on the right), allowing you to filter by a different option.

Tap the blue Filter symbol again to turn off any filtering.

Where are the rest of my emails?

If you are not 'filtering' your email using the above option - but find that you still can't see all the emails that you know are stored by your mail provider - it may be that your mail is being 'filtered' in your Mail Settings, in **Settings -> Accounts & Passwords**.

(For some accounts, you must log into your account from a web browser and adjust the sync settings from there, instead of from your iPhone/iPad. It is worth checking first, though, if you can adjust this from your device.)

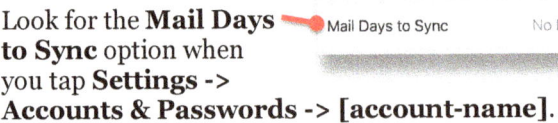

Look for the **Mail Days to Sync** option when you tap **Settings -> Accounts & Passwords -> [account-name]**.

Choose one of the options shown (see image on left) - **No Limit** will sync all your accounts mail to your device.

46

Saving Photos Received in Emails

If your email contains a photo (or maybe a few photos), how do you save or share such photos?

It's simple – just touch and hold on the image in the email until the 'share' menu pops up.

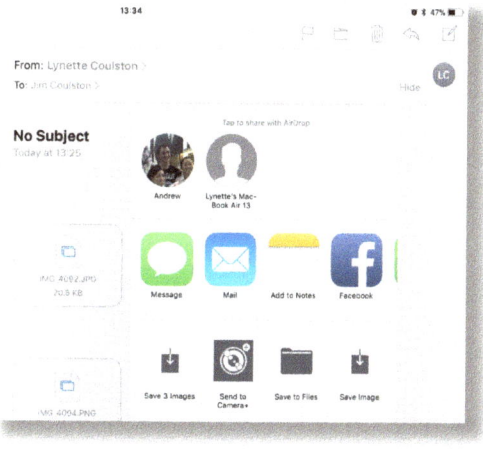

In the bottom set of options is **'Save Image'**, which saves the selected image to your Camera Roll/All Photos in the Photos app.

If there is more than one image in your email (let's say 3), there will be an option to **'Save 3 Images'**, which saves all three images to Photos.

Of course, there are also various other options available to you when you touch and hold on a photo that is in an email. You can

- Create a new mail message with that image included.
- Send it via your Message app.
- Tweet the image (if you are on Twitter).
- Share it on Facebook (if you are on Facebook).

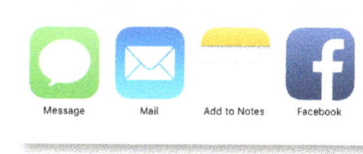

- Assign the photo to one of your Contacts (so that the photo comes up whenever that person calls).
- Print it (i.e. just print the photo, not the rest of the email).
- Copy it so that you can paste it elsewhere - into another app that allows you to include photos (for example Evernote, Pages, Notes).
- Use it in another app.

Saving Files Received in Emails

If your email contains a file of some sort, how do you save that file – and where do you save it to? For example, how do you save a PDF file containing a bill or statement to somewhere on your iPad/iPhone, so that you can access it easily later?

It's simple – just touch and hold on the attachment in the email until the 'Share' menu pops up.

Or, open the attached file by tapping on it and choose the Share option to see the same menu.

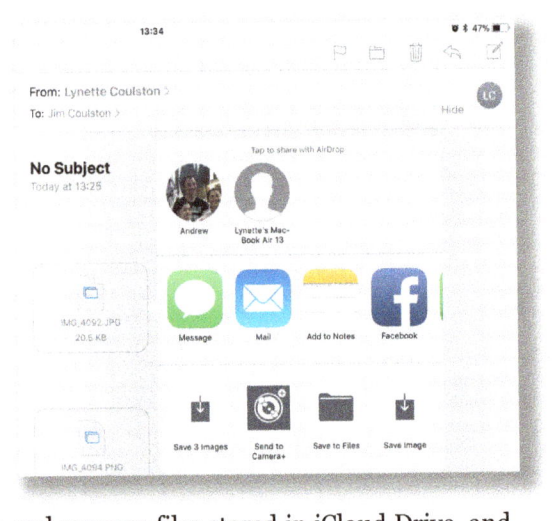

Your iPad and iPhone includes an app called the **Files** app.

If you have received some sort of file attached to your email, you will have the option to **Save to Files**.

Tap this option, then choose where to save your file – for example to your iCloud Drive.

The Files app lets you see, access and manage files stored in iCloud Drive, and in other 'cloud-based' services.

(We won't go into this App and its full capabilities here.)

PDF's can also be saved to **iBooks** and to **Notes**.

Any apps to which you can save the email's attachment will be shown along either of the rows of options.

Sending Photos and Files in Emails

There are a few ways to send your photos via email.

- Add a photo to an email while you are composing it or
- Select your photos from within the Photos app (or any other app where you have selected photos) and create an email from there.

Add Photos to an email while you are drafting it

Just touch and hold the place in your email's body where you want to add a photo, then release your finger. You will see a black bar of options appear.

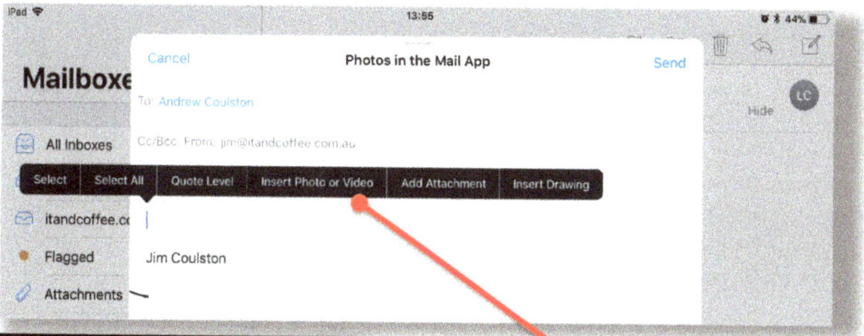

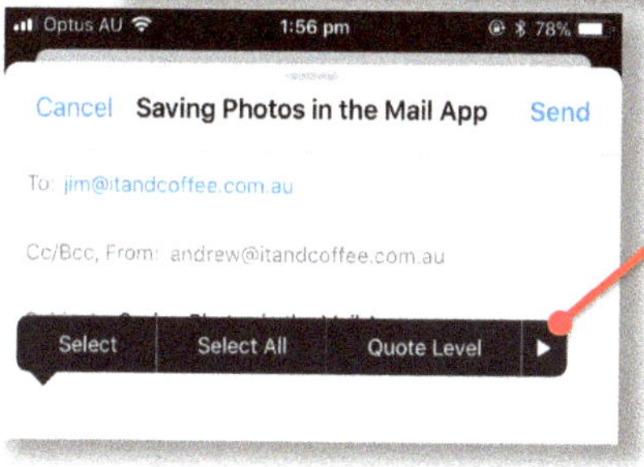

Touch on **Insert Photo or Video**.

(Note. For the iPhone, you will need to touch the ▶ at the end of the black bar to see the same option.)

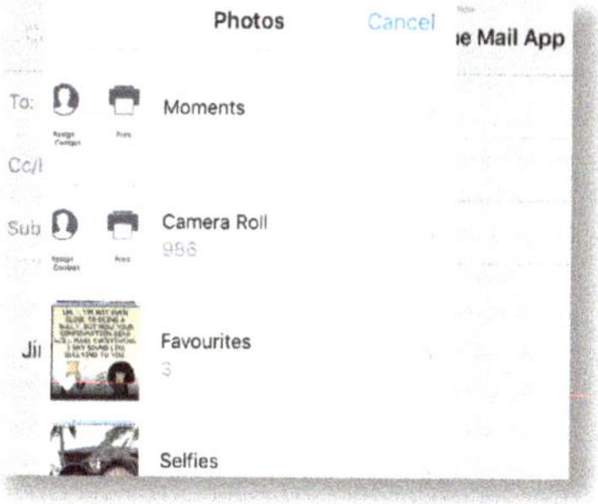

You will see a 'Photos' selection panel appear.

Just touch on the album containing the photo you want (e.g. Camera Roll or All Photos, or Moments) and find the photo.

Touch on its thumbnail to select it.

Touch Use (top right of the selected photo on the iPad) or Choose (bottom right on the iPhone) when you have found the required photo – this will pop your photo into your mail message.

Add Photo using Camera symbol on Keyboard

If you have an iPad, there is a camera symbol on the iPad keyboard – tap this, and then choose a photo from your Photos library (as described above).

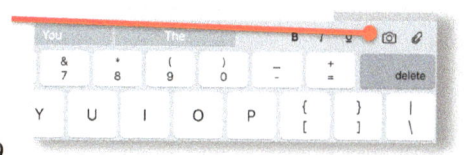

49

Sending Photos and Files in Emails

Create an email with photos from the Photos app

In the Photos app, choose the **Mail** option in the share menu ⬆ to send one or more selected photos via email. (Refer to the iTandCoffee **The Photos App on the iPad and iPhone** for details of how to select one or more photos, and how to then send them via email).

Ensure your email's images are not too large

If you send multiple images in an email, just make sure that the email you are creating is not too big to send.

Working out the size of your email differs on the iPad and the iPhone.

On the iPad, if the email will be over 500KB, you will see the size of the images in the email in the field **Images**.

Tap this word to see the options for image sizes, and the size that the email will be for each choice of image size.

Tap the size that you prefer (Small, Medium, Large or Actual Size) – I tend to go with Medium or Small, unless the person needs higher resolution versions of the photos.

This image size setting will then be 'remembered' for the next email that you send. This means that, if you adjust the size to Medium when sending a set of photos via email today, then the next time you create an email with photos, they will be automatically sized as Medium.

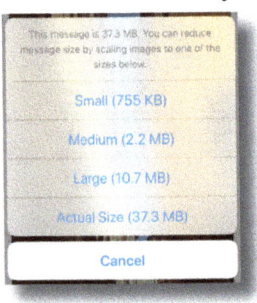

This can then be changed if you require a different sizing next time around – and will again be 'remembered'.

For the iPhone, the size of the photos that you send is not set until you hit Send.

The various size options appear (as shown on left). Once again, choose the one that you require. Once you tap the size option, your message will send.

Sending Photos and Files in Emails

Add an attachment to your email

You email can also include an 'attached file' – which could be a file of any type that is stored on your iPad or iPhone.

Follow the same steps as described for adding a photo (touch and hold on the place where the file needs to be added), but instead choose the Add Attachment option from the black bar

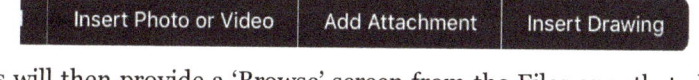

This will then provide a 'Browse' screen from the Files app, that allows you to choose the file that you would like to add. As you can guess, this means that files must be stored in the Files app (in, say, iCloud Drive) if you want to be able to add them to an email in this way.

Once again, we'll save the description of the Files App for another guide.

If you have an iPad, you may notice a paper clip next to the camera symbol. This is an alternative way to add an attached file.

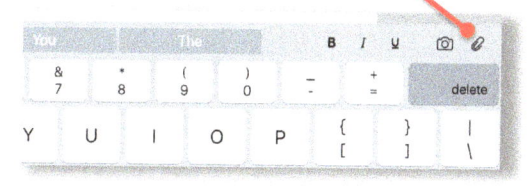

As was the case for photos, the option to share a file via email is generally available from the app's Share option.

Add a drawing to your email

As you will see in the image of the 'black bar' above, there is also the option to insert a drawing in your email!

Tap on this option, then use your finger or a stylus to draw, then press Done when you are finished to see your drawing inserted in the message at the position where you 'tapped and held'.

Removing a photo, file or drawing from your email

It is easy to remove any attachment you have added your email. Just consider the photo/file/drawing to be a single character (a number, letter or symbol) in your email. Position your cursor on the right of the item and use Backspace/Delete to remove the item.

For information about how to set your cursor position when typing and editing, refer to the iTandCoffee guide **Typing and Editing on the iPad and iPhone**.

The Importance of Contacts

Make sure you save away email addresses in Contacts

To make the most of your iPad and iPhone for keeping in touch with family, friends, and work contacts, it is important to build up an 'address book' of all your Contacts.

Contacts

Email addresses that your computer or another device know about (for example, through previous emails), but that are not in your Contacts list, will not be available on other devices and may not be available to you if you ever break or lose your device.

So, always try to save email addresses and phone numbers in **Contacts** if you want to re-use them.

The best way to build up this list is to add people's details whenever you get an email, call, or message. The details are then saved away for the next time you need to contact them.

Your list of Contacts can then be synced with other devices using iCloud (or whatever email account you choose to store your Contacts) – keeping them safe and sound, just in case something happens to your iPad or iPhone.

Saving a new email address to Contacts

You can very quickly save the details of those you contact via email (or who contact you) from within the Mail app.

To save an email address or phone number to Contacts, **just tap on the blue name in the email/text** and you will be presented with some options for what to do with this contact.

From: lynett@itandcoffee.com.au >

To: a...@andcoffee.com.au >   Hide

If the person is a new contact, choose **Create New Contact.**

The email address and (usually) the name details will be filled in for the new Contact, so that all you have to do is choose **Done**. (Change/add the first/last name details if needed.)

If you already have the person in your Contacts, but just don't have the email address recorded yet, choose **Add to Existing Contact** and select the applicable contact.

The email address will be added to the Contact.

52

A special trick for emails with event details

Sometimes you will receive an email that has details of an appointment or event that you need to get into your calendar.

There is a really quick way of popping such events into your iPad's (or iPhone's) calendar.

When you see any date and time details underlined, just touch on this to uncover some options.

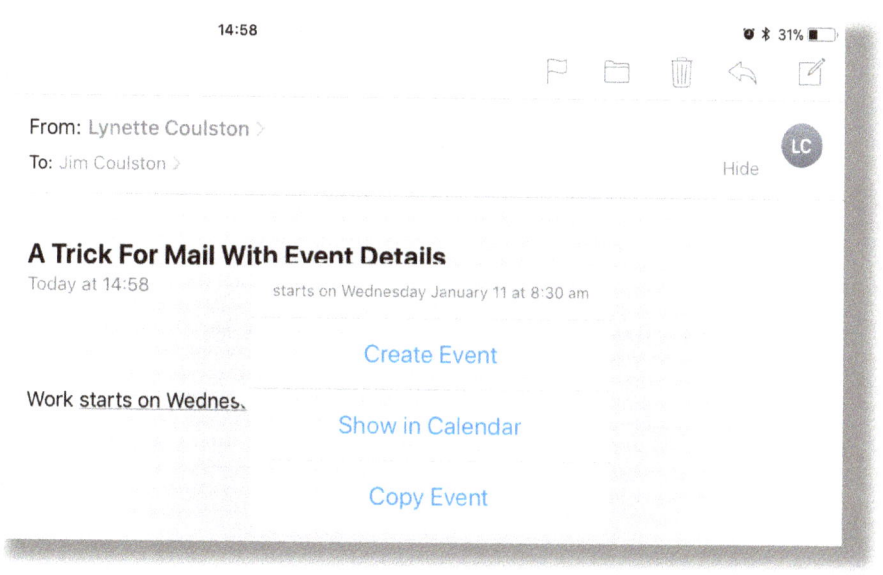

If you touch on **Create Event**, a draft event will be created, with a title usually matching your email's subject and with a date and start time based on the content of the email.

All you have to do is touch **Done** (assuming all the details are correct – modify them if you need) and your event is your Calendar!

Show in Calendar allows you to see what you have on for the date/time of the underlined email 'event'.

Filing and Organising your Mail

This is something that not everyone will be able to do – it depends on the sort of mail account that you have and how it is configured on your iPad or iPhone.

If you have an 'IMAP' or 'Exchange' mail account, you will be able to create your own **Mailboxes** to save away emails that you want to keep and easily find later. Then, when you receive an email, you will be able to move it to that mailbox using the 📁 symbol in your mail toolbar.

Creating a new mailbox

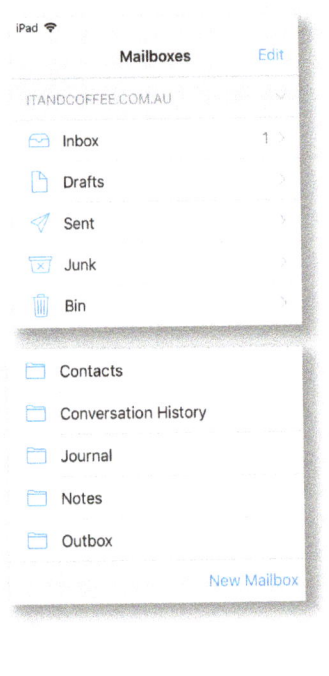

To create a new mailbox, go to your Mailboxes screen.

Tap the Edit option, and choose the New Mailbox option at the bottom of the screen (see lower image on right)

Provide a name for your Mailbox, and then touch on the **Mailbox Location** to decide where this new mailbox should reside. You can create a m ailbox hierarchy by selecting another personal mailbox as the 'parent' mailbox for the new 'child' mailbox.

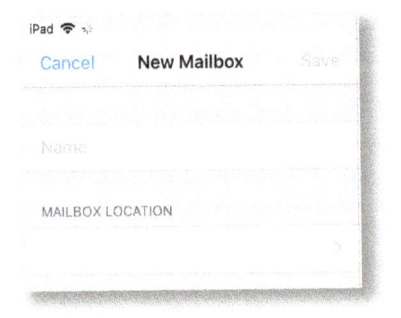

Select Save at top right after you have named your Mailbox and chosen its Location, to finish the creation of the new Mailbox.

Then, press Done to complete your Mailbox editing tasks.

Saving emails to a mailbox

Once you have created your own personal Mailboxes, you can then save any emails you receive to these Mailboxes.

When you are viewing an email, just touch on the 📁 symbol.

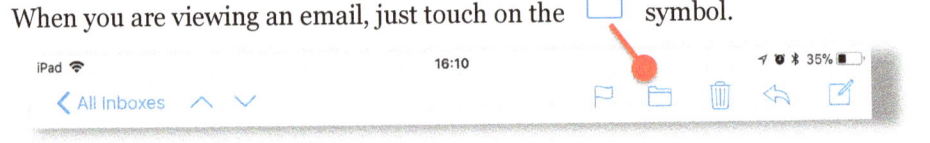

Filing and Organising your Mail

You will see a message appear at the top of the screen, telling you what to do.

Search for the mailbox into which you want to place this email.

You may need to select the option to see your different accounts and their

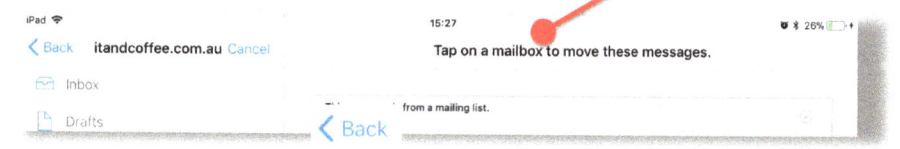

Mailboxes.

Once you have located the required mailbox, touch on it and you will see the message 'jump into' that Mailbox.

Another way to access the **Move Message** option is to swipe right-to-left on a message in the preview list, then touch the ... **More** option and choose **Move Message...**

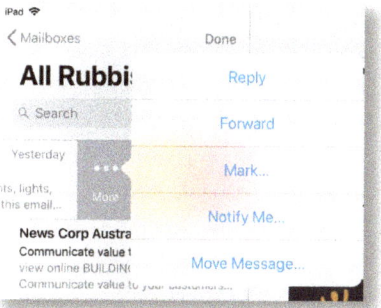

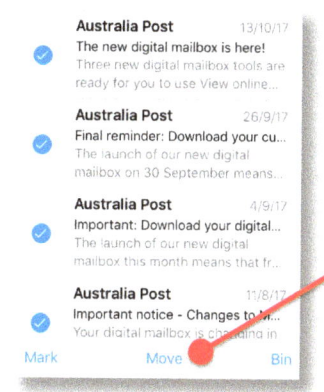

If you use the technique described earlier for selecting multiple emails (with the preview list in view, choose **Edit** and then tap several emails to select them, as shown on the left), tap the **Move** option and then choose where the new location for the selected messages.

Flagging and Marking Mail

In the tool bar at the top of your Mail message, you will see a 'Flag' symbol

Touching on this 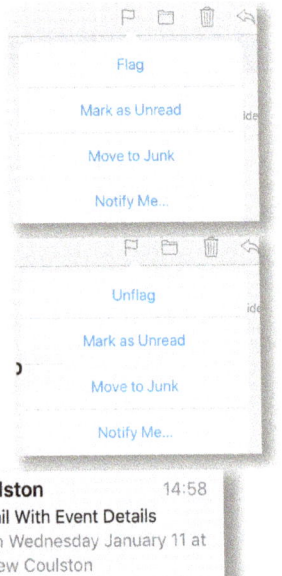 symbol allows you to do a few different things – as shown in the image on the right.

Flag an email

This option puts a 'Flag' next to a significant/ important email.

Flagged emails will appear in your mail preview list with an orange dot. If the message is unread as well, you will see an orange circle with a blue dot inside it.

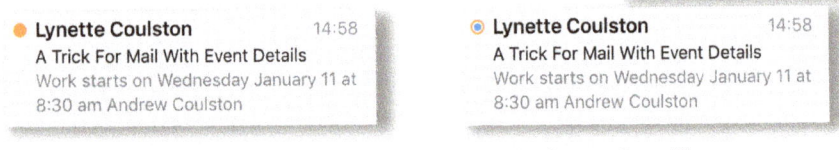

These 'flagged' emails then appear in the special **Flagged** mailbox.

Touch on that **Flagged** mailbox (as described earlier in this guide) to view all the emails that you have decided need special attention or have some other significance.

If your email is already 'flagged', the Flag symbol will let you Unflag the email, which will remove the orange dot and no longer show the email in the **Flagged** Mailbox.

Mark as unread

The 'Flag' symbol also allows you to Mark as Unread.

The email will then look as though you haven't read it (i.e. it will have a blue dot). This is handy if you want to be reminded to come back to an email and re-read it.

If the email is unread, the option here will instead be Mark as Read.

Notify Me

You can also choose a 'Notify Me' setting for the email, which is the equivalent of tapping the 'bell' symbol on the Subject field (as described earlier) – so that you receive a notification when there are any responses relating to this email.

Flagging and Marking Mail

Other ways of accessing 'Flagging' and 'Marking' options

Another way to access these same options is to swipe right-to-left on a message in the preview list, then touch the ... **More** and **Mark...**

OR

Choose **Edit** (top) when looking at your Preview list of mail, then touch on each of the messages you want to 'flag/unflag' or 'mark/unmark' and choose the applicable option at the bottom.

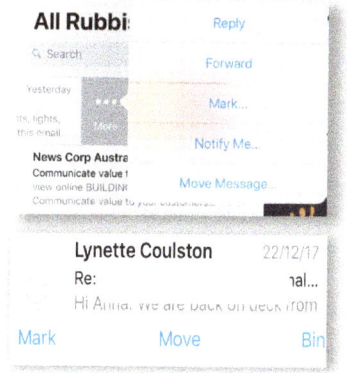

How to make a Contact a VIP

You will have noticed earlier that there is a special mailbox called your **VIP Mailbox**.

This mailbox allows you to separately see just those messages that sent to you by a select group of your email contacts – for example family and close friends, or important work associates.

So, how do you make someone a VIP?

Creating VIP from an email

Open a message from the sender you want to add to your VIP senders.

Tap the sender's name or email address in the email's header area.

Now tap Add to VIP.

This will add the email address to the list of VIP senders, but will not create a new address book entry in Contacts for the sender. (Neither will it remove an existing one, of course.)

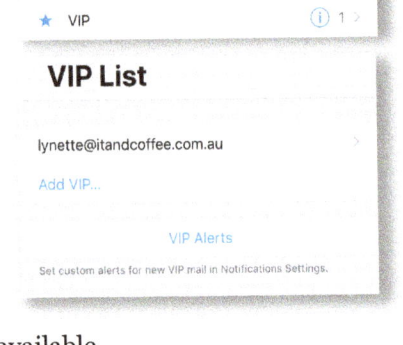

Adding a VIP from the VIP Mailbox

To add a Contacts entry to your list of VIPs, Tap the symbol ⓘ on right side of the VIP Mailbox name (in the Mailbox view).

Select Add VIP...

Your list of Contacts will appear.

Tap the desired entry from your Contacts to nominate this Contact as a VIP.

You will only be able to choose contacts for which you have an email address. Other contacts will be 'greyed' to show they are not available.

Set custom alerts for VIP emails

Also available at the bottom of the **VIP LIST** screen is the ability to set VIP Alerts.

This means you can set different sound and type of notification for VIPs (so that these types of notifications can stand out more).

These alerts are managed in **Settings -> Notifications -> Mail -> VIP**.

Some other Mail Settings

There are a few more Mail Settings worth knowing about – Settings that we have not mentioned throughout the earlier sections of this guide.

You'll find most of them in **Settings** -> **Mail**.

Ask Before Deleting

This determines whether or not you get a confirmation prompt before deleting an email.

WARNING: This doesn't get prompted if you use the 'swipe' method to delete an individual email.

Load Remote Images

Remote images are images in emails that are downloaded from websites.

If remote images are downloaded, this uses more of your data allowance.

This also lets newsletter publishers know that you have opened your emails.

It also tells spammers that you received their emails and approximately where in the world you are.

To protect your privacy and data usage, it is definitely recommended to turn this setting off.

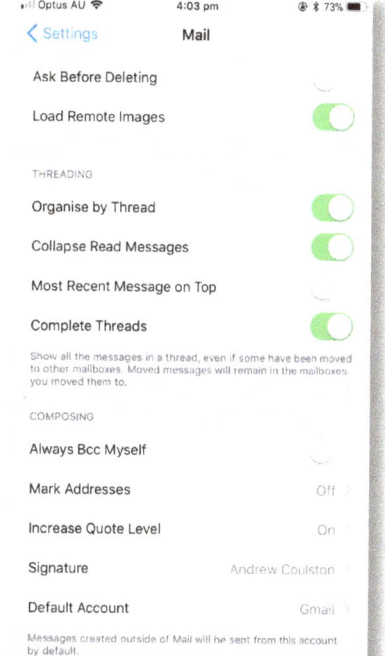

Always Bcc Myself

You can choose to 'blind copy' yourself on all emails that you send from you iPad and iPhone.

The main reason to do this would be to get any iPad/iPhone sent mail onto your computer if you have a 'Pop' account.

Increase Quote Level

When switched on, any copied text in a message that you forward or reply to is indented, with a small vertical line placed before it.

More advanced configuration settings

Change the Account's description in Mail

When you set up a new Mail account, it is allocated a default description based on the type and email address of the account.

Sometimes, it is desirable to change that default name for the account that appears in the Mail app, so that you can more easily distinguish between your email accounts.

To change the description, go to **Settings -> Accounts & Passwords** and tap on the name of the Account whose description you would like to change.

Tap on the **Account** field (i.e. the field showing your email address), then tap the **Description** field – and change the description as required.

Tap Done at top right when you are finished.

Changing 'Port Numbers' for incoming & outgoing Mail

When setting up an 'Other' type of email account, it is sometimes necessary to adjust the 'Port Numbers' for incoming and outgoing mail. We won't go into what all this means in this guide – but will just cover where to find these settings.

Go **Settings -> Accounts & Passwords** and tap on the applicable Account.

Tap on the **Account** field (the top field showing your email address).

To change the **Incoming Mail** port, tap **Advanced** and tap **Server Port** to adjust this setting. Also set SSL to on or off for incoming mail, as per on your required configuration settings.

To change the **Outgoing Mail** port, tap the **SMTP** option, then tap the top field – the PRIMARY SERVER - and tap **Server Port** to adjust this setting. Here you can also set SSL to on or off for outgoing mail, as per your required configuration settings.

Fetch vs Push settings

Another special setting can be found in **Settings -> Accounts & Passwords.** It is the **Fetch New Data** setting, found below the ACCOUNTS section.

Tap on this option to choose whether new email data will be 'Pushed' automatically to your device whenever it is available, whether it will be 'Fetched' according to a nominated schedule, or whether you would like to 'Manually' retrieve this data.

More advanced configuration settings

The only time I tend to change these settings is when I travel, to minimise data usage by Mail. I turn off **Push** and change each account to **Fetch** (instead of **Push**) and set the Fetch Schedule of **Manually.**

Then mail is only retrieved when I go into the Mail app.

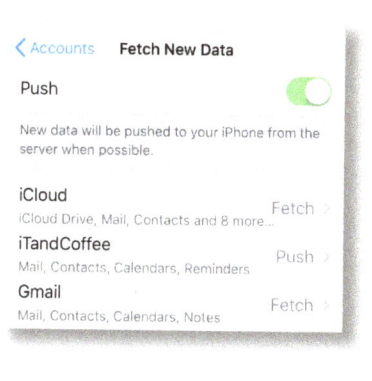
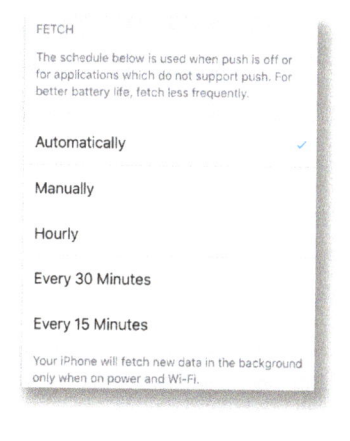

Deleting a Mail Account

If you have a mail account on your iPad or iPhone that you are no longer using, that mail account can be easily removed from your Mail app.

Go **Settings -> Accounts & Passwords** and tap on the applicable Account.

If it is an IMAP or Exchange account, and if it is just the Mail component of the account you no longer need on this device, turn off the **Mail** switch so it is no longer green.

If you no longer need any parts of that mail account on your device, you can delete it completely from your device with the **Delete Account** option at the bottom.

If the account is a POP account, you will be deleting your history of incoming and sent mail – for good (unless you restore from a backup).

If the account is an IMAP or Exchange account and that mail account is still active, you will be able to add the account again and get back all the account's mail if needed.

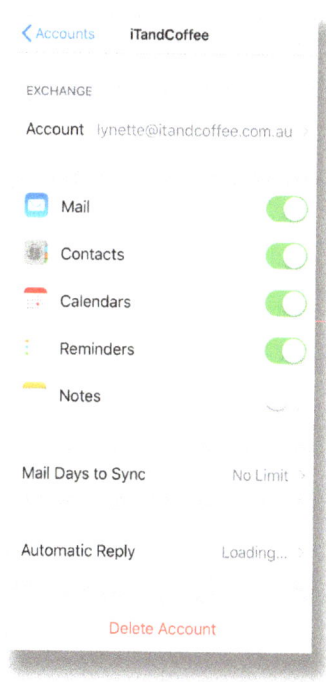

How Emails Work

First, a scary diagram!

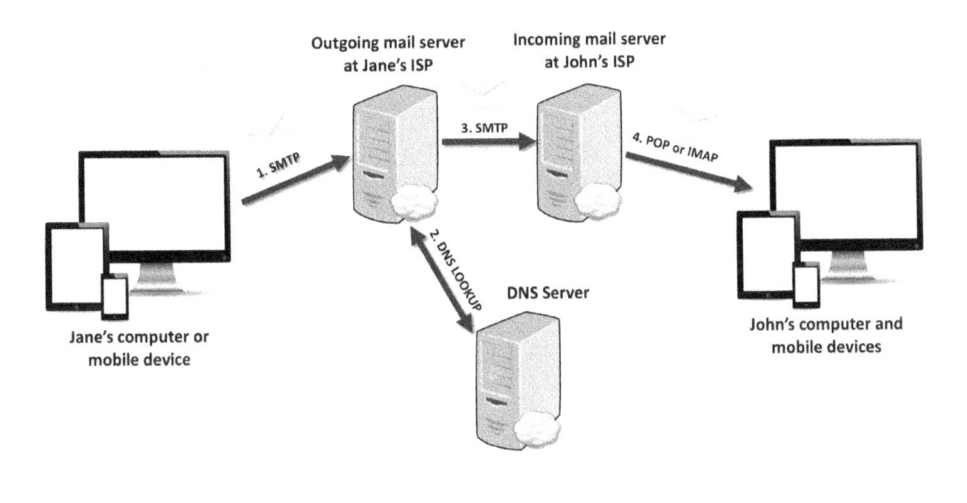

For those who are brave enough to proceed, here is a bit of an overview of how emails work, and more about the different types of email accounts.

You have an email account with your ISP (internet service provider) – for example, Telstra's Bigpond, Microsoft, iiNet, TPG, Gmail, Optusnet, Apple, Yahoo, or a privately hosted account.

In the above diagram, when Jane sends John an email, it goes via Jane's ISP - its destination is determined by the outgoing mail server of Jane's ISP.

A DNS Server provides the translation between the provided email address and the IP address of John's mail server (where the IP address is the 'internet' address of a computer/server, in the format 999.999.9.9 – eg. 158.168.0.2)

The email is then sent to John's Email Server and stored on the incoming mail server.

A **mail client** on John's computer and/or mobile device receives the email by talking to the incoming mail server of John's ISP.

(John could also access this mail directly from his web browser via his ISP's webmail page.)

The **Mail** app on your Mac, iPad & iPhone is an **email client** application.

Microsoft Outlook is another example of an **email client** and can run on a computer or on an iPad/iPhone. There are several other Apps that are Mail Clients.

The features of your email account and how you set it up depends on the type of account you have.

How Emails Work

Your ISP will provide instructions on how to configure your email account on your email client – Google is a good way of finding this information if you are not sure.

Use words like "iOS Mail settings for Bigpond" or "Optusnet outgoing mail settings for Mac".

This will help you work out how to configure the 'incoming mail server', the 'outgoing mail server' and the 'ports' that apply to incoming and outgoing mail, as well as whether to use a security feature called SSL.

Types of accounts

POP Accounts

Mail app downloads email from your ISP's server and you store the downloaded emails locally on your iPad or iPhone (or computer).

You define in Settings on your device whether to delete email from the ISP's server as soon as it is downloaded

If you set up your email client to delete immediately on download, you may not be able to retrieve the email on another device

The best approach is to set up one device to delete emails from server, but to only do this weekly/monthly so that other devices have time to retrieve the email.

Any emails you send using a Pop email account will only appear on the device from which you sent the mail.

IMAP/Exchange Accounts

Unlike POP, IMAP and Exchange accounts allow you to have two-way communication between the mail on your ISP's Mail Server and your **email client**(s).

So, when you read an email on one device, it is marked as read on your ISP's Mail Server

When you see it on another device, it will be already marked as 'read'.

Or when you delete it on one device, it will appear in the 'Trash' or 'Deleted' mail folder on another device

This provides a better method to access your mail from multiple devices.

iCloud Hotmail, Gmail, Windows Live, Outlook and Yahoo mail are automatically set up as IMAP accounts when added to your Mail app on the iPad and iPhone.

How Emails Work

Organising your IMAP email account

If your mail account is an IMAP account, you will have extra functionality available to organise your mail, something that can be done on either your computer or your mobile devices.

You can create extra folders and move received email to these folders. See our earlier section on organising your mail for how to do this.

Pop email accounts do not allow the creation of such folders from your devices.

Other Guides in the
Introduction to the iPad and iPhone
Series

* **A Guided Tour of the iPad and iPhone**

* **The Camera App**

* **The Photos App**

* **Typing and Editing**

* **Exploring the Internet on Safari**

* **Getting Organised: The Calendar App**

* **Let's Go Shopping – Getting Apps, Music, Movies, Books and more**

* **Discovering iBooks**

* **The Phone App**

* **Getting Connected**

www.ingramcontent.com/pod-product-compliance
Lightning Source LLC
Chambersburg PA
CBHW041634050326
40689CB00024B/4963